Content Copy Made Easy

How To Get More Clients and Increase Revenue

Published by Vesalius Press
This book is available at Amazon.com, https://www.createspace.com/4445762,
http://www.CompleteContentPackage.com, and other retailers.

ISBN: 0984889809
EAN-13: 9780984889808
Library of Congress Control Number: 2013951038
Vesalius Press, Boynton Beach, Florida

Content Copy Made Easy

By

Barbara Hales, M.D.

Dedication

This book is dedicated to my fellow copy-writers and content marketers. While we are down in the trenches together, we promote goods and services, explain how things function in this world and generally endeavor to improve people's lives.

Thank you to my family and friends who remain supportive.

A special thanks to AWAI, Denise Ford and Mark Morgan Ford who introduced me to "A Writer's Life", encouraged me to pursue my passion for helping others through writing, and see writing as a new career.

I would also like to thank Mike Capuzzi. His doodles have been sprinkled throughout this book. For writers that want their work to stand out, registering at www.CopyDoodles.com is a must!

Prologue

This book focuses on Content Writing and Content Marketing in its various forms.

Copywriting Vs. Content Writing- is there a difference?

This question is part of an ongoing, hot debate.

Copywriting is geared more toward selling something and content writing is more to educate or inform the reader. Because of this, the two have drifted into their own forms and many feel that content writing is more comfortable for them.

However, it seems to be quite interrelated. You can't sell copy without educating the readers and you can't provide content that is so dull that people fall asleep reading it. The writing has to be compelling or exciting, regardless of how dry a topic may be; it must hold your attention.

Since there seems to be a meshing of the two, they may not be as distinct as one may initially think. Let's coin a new phrase for the hybrid- "Content-Copy".

Perhaps the only difference is in the timing. In copywriting, you build up excitement and desire before "letting the cat out of the bag" whereas in content writing you just get straight to it.

Why is Content King?

Content Writing and content marketing is in more demand than ever before...and the demand is growing exponentially!

Websites need unique and fresh content to be added constantly and consistently. Content reflects a selected niche and key- words so that the website is ranked well by the search engines. Let's face it. Only listings on the first page of a search will be contacted. No one ever scrolls down to page 25 and contacts listings from there.

Businesses also need fresh content to attract prospective clients, garner leads, and maintain the interest of current clients. Blog posts, press releases, case studies, white papers and pub-lished articles are some of the many forms of content marketing.

How to Get Started?

First, figure out who your target market is and what benefits that you can offer them. Decide upon your goal. What is it that you want to achieve? Content marketing can help with:

- Lead generation

- Lead conversion

- Strengthening Brand

- Establishing Authority/Celebrity in a Field

- Offer solutions to problems that your target market is struggling with

Knowing whom your market is and what the goal of your content marketing is will help set the tone and how you are going to be captivating. Get into the minds of your audience. What are they interested in? What do they want to know?

What form of content marketing will best achieve the goals that you have set out?

With this in mind, you are now ready to see the types of content marketing and the intricacies involved with them to help you on the road to success.

Table of Contents

Search Engine Optimization

SEO
MADE EASY

Chapter 1
SEO

SEO: What it is and Why You need it

Studies show that business or practices that have a website, succeed more than twice that of companies lacking one. Optimizing this site is vital for your success.

Effective SEO practices start right from the beginning with the choice of the domain name.

What is SEO?

SEO is an acronym for search engine optimization. It is a process of writing that enables search engines like Google or Yahoo to identify websites, blogs and other online content, ranking it for meeting its criteria.

In working within SEO guidelines, web- sites can improve their quality, making it faster and easier to navigate, as well as becoming more user-friendly as it helps viewers quickly identify what the site is all about primarily.

Why YOU need it

Quite simply, ranking higher with SEO enriched content helps you get noticed.

Don't think this is an advantage?

Just check out these statistics.

As of December 2012:

- Number of websites- 634 million

- Added websites in 2012- 51 million

- WordPress sites- 59.4 million

- Tumblr blogs- 87.8 million

- Page views for Tumblr- 17.8 billion

- Visitors to Google Sites- 191 million

- Reddit.com page views- 37 billion

- Web pages run by WordPress viewed monthly- 3.5 billion

These billions of pages and sites are creating an explosive noise through which you are trying to be heard!

Now, would you like to edge them out and be #1?

The problem is getting higher rankings.

The solution is SEO.

The result- appearing on the first page of searches and... BEING FOUND!

Users are most apt to do business with those companies found within the first few listings on the first page of their search.

Perhaps at this point you are shaking your head and saying that with billions of competitors, it is not possible to make a breakthrough.

The thing to remember is that while there are billions of websites, there are not billions within your niche, your type of business and your type of market.

Search engines are seeking sites that provide answers to the problems being sought by people they are serving. SEO allows them to perform this function.

By keeping a close eye on optimizing your site, blog, ezine or etail store, you can simultaneously meet your business plan, objectives and rapid growth.

Chapter 2
Rankings

Search engines rank sites according to complex algorithms, which are changing constantly so that no one person or group can have an advantage to the "secrets" by which they boost websites or businesses. Panda was one of the more recent sets of criteria. Now there is Hummingbird.

However, there are certain important adjustments that you can make to your website for increased visibility. These involve building outside links to your site and your website structure.

Links

All links are not built equally. Bad or negative links are those that are purchased or coming from link farms. Good or positive links are those that are arising from well- known sites. These links are evidence of trust, which search engines look for in determining which are the most val-ued webpages.

Having good content on your website or blog will naturally create links as people are looking for the helpful answers that you provide.

Website Structure for SEO

Imagine the experience visitors have when com-ing to your site. A site must be easy to navigate. It's one that is planned in a specific sequence.

Designing a website in an optimal fashion is a craft that you will learn in the next chapter.

Chapter 3
Creating an Optimal Website

The IDEAL website is:

- Inviting

- Informative

- Inbound Link savvy

When a visitor comes to the site, it should be obvious as to:

- what the content is

- what the purpose of the content is

- How to navigate the site

- How to get to each page with one or two clicks

- How to contact the business

Keyword stuffing will take away from the user experience and make the site difficult to read or understand. One must be mindful of highlighting keywords within the body of the website.

Stuffing is using the set of chosen keywords in an inordinate amount of times within the given content, irrespective of the flow and meaning so that reading, (now an abnormal way for someone to express themselves) becomes difficult.

6 Key Structural Development Issues for Websites

1) **URL (domain address)-** showcases the keywords.

   When you are starting out, no one is searching for your name. They are searching for a specific subject, a type of widget, a location, and a type of business. By having this in your domain name, your website pops up first. In other word, by putting key- words in the name that reflect you or your business, the name is doing the work for you in capturing views.

2) **Category**

   By making titles and category names rich in keywords, you are helping to optimize your site.

3)   Title Tag

This is an opportunity to use descriptive and helpful names. Since this is what appears as a headline on search results, you want the title to be compelling, enticing and informative.

Viewers should feel that by clicking on your website, they will get the solution to their problems or glean the information that they have been surfing.(a site that they simply must read!)

When the title tag not only has an enticing, great headline, but also has the right keywords to increase search engine rankings, you have a winning combination for users to read and bookmark.

4)   Linkage

Analyze which of the pages on your websites receive the most links. Direct these links to internal pages within the site containing fresh content to gain publicity or to get quoted.

5)   Internal Page Content

Visitors may view various pages on the website without navigating through the planned sequence starting with the home page. Thus, each of the web pages must be optimized for the chosen keywords and have informative, helpful, and interesting content.

6)   Sharing is Caring

Make sure that your viewers can share the information that they find on your site. Have icons for an RSS feed and the social media sites that you participate in. Each icon should be hyperlinked so that with one click, the viewer is giving you a "vote for popularity" and showing others that your site is the one to visit and read.

Chapter 4
What is Good SEO Writing?

Good SEO writing puts a face and voice to the body of content.

Think about it for a moment. Without a face and voice, could a person be identified? Of course not! This is needed for recognition. The same holds true for SEO writing. It's needed so that people know who you or your business is and what you're all about.

Long gone are the days where just having a website meant people would see the landing page and read about the goods and services.

There are thousands of websites springing up every day. Millions of online sites are hawking their wares. Without good SEO writing, or search engine optimization, a person or company will be lost in the sea of websites, wandering aimlessly about.

Identify SEO Goals

What is it that you want to accomplish with your site? Is it to educate? Is it to get leads with new clients?

Good SEO writing can accomplish this while directing traffic to your site and getting the traffic to convert to valued clients.

Take time to identify keywords that describe who and what you do. Good SEO writing incorporates these keywords into your content. Then, when people search these keywords, your site pops up.

Optimizing your site with good SEO writing also allows the search engines to understand and recognize who you are. The virtual spiders and search robots that crawl through the World Wide Web, find you with the keywords that you identified, and link you to the people who do the search. The more this occurs, the higher your ranking will rise and the more visible you will be.

It is crucial to keep in mind with your quest for good SEO writing that "stuffing" is frowned upon.

Stuffing is when keywords are loaded onto a web page in the site maps, Meta tags or a web page itself. Repetition of these words can make the page unreadable or unnatural to the way we speak.

Not only does this unethical technique fail to increase rankings, the keyword stuffing can lead to being barred from major search engines. This is definitely not good SEO writing!

Ensuring that your website and content incorporates good SEO writing can be very time-consuming but is crucial to the success of your site. It's the single most important key to identifying you, establishing your authority, bringing you traffic and giving you new leads.

If this is not for you, outsource it. There are many good SEO writers just waiting for your call!

Chapter 5
Benefits

Creating good content that's written with search engine optimization makes the site easier to navigate for both users and search engines.

But making the site more user- friendly is only one of many benefits.

7 SEO Advantages

1) Boosts Ranking

Identifying keywords that represent you, your business, products and services is crucial- not only for you but for search engines.

When these keywords are used consistently, they are identified and recognized by the search engine spiders that crawl the Internet.

Search engines then equate your website with these keywords and increase your ranking for the terms.

Keep in mind that higher rankings translate to being on the first page of search results.

2)   Strengthens Brand

Let's face it. When a search is performed online, people don't usually go beyond the first and maybe the second page of the responses to their request.

Companies that are listed first are perceived to be more highly valued for the services they offer.

3)   Captures   leads   and   Increases Conversions

Optimized sites receive not just random increased visits but targeted views by those who are looking specifically for your goods and services. They are ready and eager to learn more from you, and get what you have to offer. They are much more apt to become subscribers, fans and customers.

4)   Increases Social Media engagement

Everyone wants to be connected to a winner- the one who

- ranks the best

- consistently provides the most sought after news-breaking or useful information

- has the best reputation

After all, association with the best puts you in a good light too!

Having a high search ranking will garner more exposure. This is self-fulfilling.

The higher the ranking, the more social connections there are which creates more links and increases ranking. This promotes more connections and more links, which creates greater exposure. See how the practice of SEO helps growth exponentially?

5)   Increases Traffic

Just like any numbers game, the more people that view your site and see what they are looking for, the more likely these same people will click on your site for more information.

In turn, the increased traffic will dramatically grow your fan base, and your subscription rates to newsletters, ezines and blogs. Usage of your services will increase and purchases of your products will soar.

6)   Smashes Competition

The business that has visibility will outdo the same type of business that is not seen or noticed, by far. An optimized business will grow exponentially, getting more traffic and leads while leaving the competition lacking an optimized site in the dust!

7)   Works for you 24/7 as a Promoter

Unlike you and your business, the virtual world never sleeps and never closes, working around the clock, 7 days of the week.

Your website works for you even when you don't!

When perspective clients and customers go online searching for your keywords and it is you that pops up on their screen, your website works for you by pointing them in your direction- a great promotion for your business.

This far exceeds the sporadic press releases and ads that you pay for and is far more consistent.

Chapter 6
How To Optimize a Site
(Or how to choose the right keywords)

7 Tips to choosing the best keywords

1)   Think like your client

The first step in selecting the keywords that will work most effectively is to put yourself in the shoes of your ideal client.

What words would this person key in when doing a search (that also describes you or your business)

2)   Use long-tail keywords

Combine 2-3 words together as a descriptive phrase for your products or services. Make them specific but not so technical that a person who is not in the trade can still understand and still be apt to search these words.

Don't make them too vague or generic because you will then be competing with everyone in that genre. The trick is in the balance so that they search for a topic and you stand out, leading the pack.

3) Look at Your Website

Ask yourself, "What are all the topics that I provide solutions for?" "What words could be used that describe each product, service or feature"?

4) Look at Your Location

If you are a brick and mortar business, having your geographical location of your business listed, works very well. When people are searching for a type of non-virtual business, most will search for the company that is closest to them. E.G. Instead of plumber, one would look for "Hartford, Connecticut Plumber".

5) Look at Your Competition

See what other businesses are using for keywords in your niche, for ideas. Find them in the keyword tags (which you can find under source in the View tab of your browser)

6) Be Keyword Savvy

Using a keyword tool to run your selections through, is vital to success. While you may have chosen the words, which seem perfect, your clients may not have the same mind frame. Entering your keywords in these programs will confirm how effective they are.

Not only will keyword tool programs show how effective the keywords you entered are, these programs will also suggest word combinations that most people search for so that you can add these to your list for consideration.

7) Use an analytical program

The keywords that you have chosen are not etched in stone. Search engine optimization for your site is an ongoing process.

By using an analytical program, you can see which words received the most attention and which words got no visits. You can then adjust your list accordingly until the results are satisfactory.

While in the investigative stage, you may want to enroll in a pay-per-click program for a nominal investment per month, which will tell you how many impressions are received for each keyword you are working with. When the results become blatant, you can continue with a free analytical program (e.g. Google Analytics Tool)

Chapter 7
Keyword Search Tools

Until the budget is available for ongoing research, there are free search sites that you can visit for your initial assessment.

Sites with Free Keyword Searches

http://www.Webmeup.com

Although this is a paid site, they offer a 15-day free trial. Webmeup is an extremely helpful source, which provides video guides for training, community resources, instruction on how to get started with SEO tools and keyword research. In addition, there is a knowledgebase for perusal where an FAQ is located along with features, terms and helpful tips.

http://www.SEMRush.com

This is a paid site with a free option that also displays the metrics for Google search results. It offers related keywords. Retrieve list of Google and AdWord keywords for any site.

http://www.keywordeye.co.uk

This site originates in Great Britain so some terms may be particular to them. An advantage is that searches bear results in several languages if your business functions globally. Another great feature is that it provides a Cloud visualization that highlights all the keywords in that particular niche or surrounding the chosen keyword entered.

Although this is a paid site, there is a free option that limits the user to 100 keywords.

http://www.keywordspy.com

This site is both useful and fun as it allows you to "spy on company keywords". Enter a domain into the search box and they will supply you with the amount of money that the company invested in paid search for each keyword and the ones that their competitors used. They also show paid competitors and organic competitors for comparison.

The free version is limited to 10-20 entries per tab on their site.

http://www.wordpot.com

This free tool generates niche keywords. The amount of searches is limited in the free version as the company attempts to upsell to the paid plan.

http://www.keyworddiscovery.com

Tool, made by Trelian Software, compiles keywords from more than 200 major search engines globally to produce one of the largest collections of searched keywords.

http://www.addons.mozilla.org

This is a keyword generator available as an extension from Firefox. When entering a specific word, the generator retrieves it on every page and displays the frequency with which the word appears and the average position. Data from this plugin tells which keywords are strong on each web page visited.

http://www.nichebot.com

This free tool accesses the database from word tracker and gives information on rank functions with its keyword analysis.

Google also offers free tools for site optimization. Take advantage of it!

1) Google Analytics

Not only measures your sales and conversions, it displays your visitors' actions to see what pages on your website are doing well and which has no or few views. Adjustments can then be made accordingly.

2) Google Webmaster Tools

Here you can see how Google indexes your site and the top searches that drove traffic.

3) Google Insights for Search

Compare search volume across times, geographical areas and categories for each set term or long-tailed keywords. Discover customers based on search volume.

4) Google Alerts

After entering a keyword into this tool, any place on the web where this keyword is talked about (blogs, articles, newsletters, web pages) will pop up in your inbox.

Designation of volume or type of information that you want is possible. Seeing the amount and type of email results lets you know how popular a keyword or phrase is in your target market.

5) Google Adwords

Discover which keywords will get the most leads to your site with this tool.

6)   Google Trends

See what's hot in the market currently. This tool shows the most popular search terms in a given niche. Contrast the trends for several keywords or sites. See trends in keyword campaigns to achieve maximum success.

If you are writing SEO copy for a business other than your own, there are certain key questions to enable you to choose the ideal keywords. Bear in mind of course that if you are choosing for yourself, the same queries apply.

Questions

- How do you describe your business?

- What words best depict your services or products?

- What problems do you solve?

- Which of the products are most profitable?

- What keywords do YOU think describe you?

Write down 15 key phrases that answer the questions above and then explore these out with the keyword search tools.

Chapter 8
Keyword Locations

Once keywords are chosen, it is time to use them prominently.

1. Page Titles

The head or start of each page must have its own title with a brief description of the page contents so that the viewer understands what the page is about. (E.g. About page or Bio talks about the person or company with the salient features including mission statement or prior achievements)

2. Home Page

This is the first or main page of a website and depicts what the website and person or business is all about. Navigation bars are found here to surf the site.

3.   Blog Posts

Each blog post should be written with SEO in mind. Rather than writing about topics randomly, the posts should center on subjects dealing with your keywords. This helps not only for ranking but also to let your audience know what it is that you represent, and what types of problems you solve.

4.   Newsletter

Articles, often taken from blog post collections, should also focus on the keywords that represent you and the ones that your readers have come to expect.

5.   Registration with distributing sites

Syndicate your blogs, ezines and newsletters by registering with various distributing sites. Keywords are used to describe what category your written material covers.

6.   Bylines

Typically 3 lines that describes the author of an article or any other publication, bylines can be found at the end of a written piece or between the headline and start of an article.

Placing keywords here will target additional traffic to your site when searches are done on a specific topic.

7.   Resource Box

Appearing at the end of an article, it is a "box" that mentions the author's name, bio, details and hyperlink to a website, book or product landing page.

The resource box enables self-promotion and essentially allows mention of your call to action. (what ever you want the viewers to do) Typically it is restricted to 3-5 lines.

Bear in mind that there should be a link to your website's home page since building backlinks to this page is crucial in driving traffic and capturing leads. (Backlinks are connections back to your site)

Chapter 9
Chain reaction

It is vital to build links for a strong chain to your website. But not all links are the same.

Link Types

- **Internal Links**

    Connections that show a relationship to other pages within a website, internal links redirect a reader to another page within the site for more information.

    Internal links are associated through key-words to enable easier navigation by the viewer. Limit the links to 5 per page.

Sporadically, links can be added, connecting old blog posts or archived ezine articles to newer ones, highlighting and strengthening given information material.

- **Back Links**

    Also known as inbound links, they are connections to a web page from an external source. These help website rankings considerably and can be developed through article publishing and guest blogging as well as through social media.

     Do not "buy" back links as many offer to sell for ranking improvement. Search engines recognize this process and frown upon it. Penalties result in the form of lowering your web page rankings.

Chapter 10
Tips and Key Information

➢ An optimized website is crucial for business success. Results of a Google survey show that a business using the web effectively grows 40% more than the competition.

➢ Keyword selection is paramount in identifying your business, products and services. Choose long-tail keywords and optimize the URL or domain name as well.

➢ Optimization= Publicity and Promotion = Success

Use keywords on every piece of writing from the business, which includes brochures, mailings, newsletters, blogs.

➢ Businesses that have higher rankings garner more trust and are perceived to be of much higher value.

➢ SEO is a continuous process. Websites need fresh content constantly as rankings are always being reevaluated and valued. This fresh content needs to be optimized.

➢ Adding content without a plan is like running a race on a treadmill.

➢ Use a keyword search tool to add valuable words to your list to attract more customers or clients.

➢ Don't forget to add location-descriptive keyword (e.g. state or city) if you have a brick and mortar business.

➢ Do not choose the most competitive keywords as it will be much harder to get noticed in the crowd and will take much longer to rank well.

Chapter 11
Review

Answer these questions to review what you've learned.

1) What is SEO?

2) What are long-tailed keywords?

3) What is keyword stuffing?

4) Name at least 4 benefits of SEO and explain why.

5) List questions to consider when choosing keywords.

6) Why is it important to optimize a website?

7) What are internal and external links? What are the difference and the benefits?

8) How do you get external links?

9) What would you hope to get by using a search engine tool?

10) What is a resource box and what con- tent would you put in it?

Chapter 12
Review Writing Blogs Effectively
How To Seize Attention and Entice
Readers to Come Back

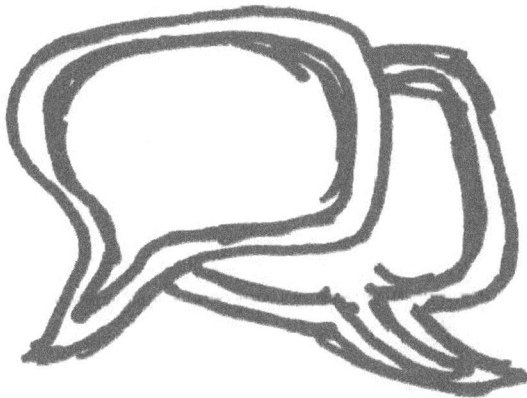

There is so much more to blogging than just offering a creative way to express and publish news, notes and ideas. While blogs do provide an avenue for engaging customers and audiences, the site supplies content online that search engines can index.

Before happily trotting off to start the blog posts, a strategic plan must be mapped out for maximum effect. Otherwise, the spiders and bots will not recognize you, your fans will not find you, and it will be a waste of time.

Chapter 13
Plan of Action

The backbone of blogging strategy involves:

- **SEO (search engine optimization)**

  Focus your posts around certain keywords, which tell not only people but also search engines like Google, but also what you represent. This way, Google selects your blog when people are searching to find what they want in your category.

- **Keywords**

  Think about which words people use to search for your post and include them in the body text and headers. It's important to make sure that your keyword placement is natural and does not seem out of place.

Long- tail keywords, which garner more attention, are 3 or 4 words strung together that make the search more specific. An example of this is beginner's lessons for classical guitar. Right away, people interested in this will hone in on your site and you eliminate advanced musicians or those that enjoy hard rock.

Keywords should reflect what the company represents so that those searching will find the business right away.

Keyword stuffing is a cardinal sin in blogging. Not only is it unethical, but also will evoke search engine penalties that greatly hurt your search rankings.

Simply put, keyword stuffing is taking the keywords that you have chosen and placing them into the body of your blog content in an inordinate amount of times so that it is noticed.

Unfortunately, doing so often makes the content unreadable or nonsense to the viewer. Therefore, DON'T DO it! Instead, create a new page for each keyword that you would like to utilize.

- ## Editorial Schedule Mapping

THINK AND DECIDE
WHAT YOUR GOALS ARE
BEFORE YOU TAKE ACTION

Decide how frequently the blog posts will appear. The number of times in a month that posts are put up is not as important as the consistency of it.

However, a well-known blogger, Michael Stelzner, founder of TheSocialMediaExaminer.com recommends that you should strive for 3 times a week. The reason behind it is that most people will only read a blog for the first 3 days of posting. Fresh content must be posted again to keep the viewers coming back.

You are training your readers to go to your site and eagerly await your next post. If you don't post on the same days or ignore the posting for a while, you will not only disappoint your fans, you will actually discourage them from coming back. After all, you are not the only site in the blogosphere.

Decide on which days you will be posting and also on which days certain topics will be covered. Make a map or schedule of how the month will be so that you can stay consistent. Perhaps one day will be dedicated to FAQs, another to products and still another to what is going on in your field.

If the blog is established for a company, each member of the company can be assigned a day or topic to lighten the burden of blogging frequency.

A planning worksheet can be downloaded from www.Scribd.com.

- **Goals**

SCHEDULE KEYWORDS
AND TOPICS FOR EACH DAY
REFLECT READER INTEREST

There are several purposes to blogs such as:

- Lead generation- getting new clients and customers

- Establishing authority in a field of expertise

- Getting name and brand recognition without expensive advertising campaigns

- Becoming the go-to person for solutions to problems that your target market suffers with

- Building a chat room or online community

- Publishing articles to compile for book publication in the future

- **Topics**

  Posting engaging content entices people to share the information over their sites. This is when it goes "viral", spreading like wildfire over the Internet across multiple social sites.

  Topics that are read the most fre- quently touch upon current events, fads, celebrities, controversies in the news or solutions to problems that your target market is strug- gling with.

  Blogs should not talk about your company or you. It is supposed to be engaging, enter- taining and educational. If your blog is a self-serving advertisement, readers will never come back and you will be ranting on a soapbox alone in a dark room with no one to see or hear.

- **Guest Blogging**

  There really are many types of blogs but most are considered personal, corporate blogs or special interest blogs. Most blogs offer commentary, but can also be used to communicate news and information.

  Blogs are a great way for you to share what you know, feel and what you want others to know.

  Interviewing people who have valuable information to share with your readers makes you more interesting and helpful, adding content to your site.

  Permit others to blog on your site as well. This will not only form strong strategic bonds with them, it will also give you a break!

- **Links**

  Guest posting is a great way to get links or when other viewers come to your site. Avoid buying links at all costs. Search engine bots and experts are trained to spot when this occurs. Your site will be flagged and penalized.

Linking to unrelated sites or categories also flags irregular activity and is frowned upon.

- **Copycat Posts**

  Don't post duplicate content whether it is from another site or even your own. Not posting original content will cause search engine penalties. Instead, you can refer back to original posts and expand upon it.

Chapter 14
Some more about Blogs...

You may have heard of it before but there are many different types and styles of blogs including written word blog, video blogging and photo blogging.

Including multimedia in your blogs like videos and images can get the audience's attention, which is important in today's society of short attention spans.

People's comments alone can actually help promote your blog to other audiences. Many different commenting systems allow users to share their comments on Networks like Facebook or Twitter while leaving a link there to the original blog post. The link opens up invites for others to join in the conversation on your blog and exposes you to more people.

Blogs tend to be interactive by giving your audience the chance to leave comments on every post. This is what causes many social media types to say that blogging is about a "conversation." You respond in return and there's a two-way exchange, or conversation, happening on the blog.

Yes, having a blog is a time commitment. Ask yourself if you have the time to manage a blog yourself.

Decide why it is that you want to have a blog! Whether it is for personal reasons, passion for a topic or for your business, spend some time doing some research by reading blogs of all types and decide what blogs you are drawn towards.

Chapter 15
Getting Started

Now that you have a goal in mind, a niche or theme that you have selected, choose your domain name and register it. There are several places to do so but the most commonly used company to register the name is http://www. GoDaddy.com/. Type in the name, and they will let you know if it is available.

Another registry is http://www.Namecheap. com. This site is cheap as the name implies and the support is also very good. Their interface is also easy to use.

You would be amazed at how many people choose the same name or variations of it, so when you find a name that you like and you are lucky enough to have it available, GRAB IT! If you don't, someone else surely will.

Many active online users will have a whole array of names. Though not all of them may be used, they own the name to prevent others from using them and it will always be available, when the time is right.

Now that you have a name, it's time to select your host, which is the one that will be serving your site. Web hosting is simply where your blog sits online.

Chapter 16
Hosts

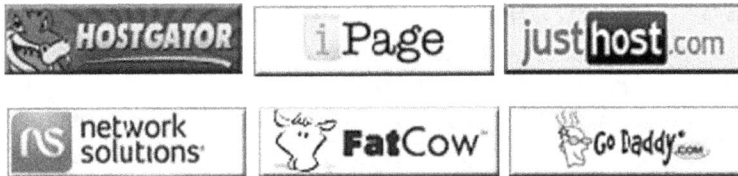

Blue Host

Inexpensive, this site offers great round-the-clock support. Your blog can be installed with one simple click.

In addition to Blue Host, the top 5 most popular host servers, chosen for low price, ease of use and feature-rich service are:

- Ipage

- Justhost.com

- Network solutions

- Fatcow (this one gives a free domain name - $8-12 savings)

- GoDaddy

Platforms

- **Wordpress**

  Most commonly used platform, WordPress offers a wide array of plugins and themes to customize your blogs and the support system is exemplary. Knowing HTML and coding is not necessary. Once you are registered, write a post and hit publish. WordPress takes care of the rest!

  Note that there is a WordPress.com and WordPress.org. The first one is free and the second has a fee, which comes with additional options for the more advanced and adventurous blogger.

  ### New blog page vs. new blog post

  Posts are the current weekly entries onto your site and are listed in reverse chronological order with the most recent one on top.

  Pages are devised for the static content such as your bio or information about yourself and your website. It is not meant to be part of conversations and as such do not participate in the RSS feed.

A comparison can be made as such:

Posts	Pages
• Current	Static
• Interactive	Personal,
• Categorized	Classified

- **Blogger**

  Operates from a site provided by Google for you. Although you are allowed to link your blog page to your website here, blogger does not run from your own website directly. In addition, there are some themes or plugins that you may want which cannot be used.

- **TypePad**

  TypePad also restricts the ability to use plugins and installation of themes that you may want for your blog.

Chapter 17
Key Metrics

LOOK AT THE ROI
FROM YOUR BLOGS!
GOOD JOB TEAM!

It is crucial that you have a method to measure the success of your blog post. Then you can eliminate what does not work and refine those techniques that do for the readers in your niche.

Discover:

- Who is referring your traffic? (Is it social media, search engines, guest blogs or other sites)

- Where is your traffic coming from?(Is it local, regional, foreign)

- Which topics get the most views?

- How many times do viewers come before signing up?

Chapter 18
Plug Ins

Plugins are tools that expand the functionality of the platform that you have chosen for your blog. They enable customization of features and functions to personalize the blog site to explicit needs.

If you are creative and want to produce your own plugin, there is a wide-ranging re- source list in WordPress Plugin Resources. (http://codex.wordpress.org/Plugin_ Resources)

- **Akismet**

    Spam blocker system that prevents your blog and comments from being overrun by autobots.

- **All in One SEO Plugin-** Enables the blog owner to select what will show at the top of the browser for your site. This information is used in search results.

- **DiggDigg-** Enables you to place the icons for social media sharing on each blog (e.g. Google+, Facebook like box, twitter, LinkedIn)

- **Google Site Map-** Provides a map of all your archived blog posts and pages

- **Retweet–** allows readers to tweet your blog to their followers

- **WPtouch-** removes all the graphics to make blog posts easily visualized and user-friendly for those using mobile devices

- **Live Chat-Casengo-** Customer Support Software offering social media, email and live chat from the cloud.

- **FAQ & Knowledge Base Plugin-** Powered by Casengo, it offers a highly recommended Knowledge Base and FAQ on websites and WordPress Blogs.

Chapter 19
Get Found

1) **Register** your blog on a free repository site so that it can be categorized and seen by the masses as it climbs the ranks. It is as easy as entering the blog URL into the registry. The most well-known of these sites is Technorati.

2) **Enable Viral Sharing-**connect your posts to your social media sites

3) **Activate RSS Feeds-** **(Real SImple Syndication)** enables readers to register your blogs like opt-ins to instantly get any new posts that you create.

4) **Install email opt-in-** enables readers to get on a list so that they continue to receive your blogs without seeking it each time. The value however, is in the list for you so that if you have any announcements, changes, promotions or sales, you can send the breaking news or

message to everyone on this list. They are already interested in what you have to say!

5) Ping.fm- allows account-holders to cross post on several social media outlets.

6) HootSuite-

Enables control of social media by allowing scheduling of blog posts, integrates other social media sites and analyzes campaigns.

Chapter 20
Key Points

How to make your blog post effective:

1) Call to action

What do you want your visitor to do? Is it comment in the box below, subscribe to a newsletter, opt-in to the blog post itself or some other action?

You can't assume that the reader knows what you want. You must actually tell the person visiting your site how to navigate it and choose the action that you have in mind.

2) Interact with your readers.

Just as in forums or chat rooms, people who leave comments would like to know that they are posting to real humans and that the comments are being read. Speak to them as friends.

You will acquire loyal fans and be rewarded with higher search engine rankings as an additional reward!

Tell stories that illustrate the key points that you would like to convey. People re- member stories long after any advice that you impart. Ask questions to encourage responses or com- ments from the readers.

3) Google Analytics

This should be installed as soon as the blog site is established. Google analytics enables the blogger to monitor the site and see what works (keywords, content, design) If there is no inter- est in a particular topic, blog more about the ones that garner more attention.

Sync the blog with AdSense and Analytics to get statistics so that you have proof to claims of rankings, clicks and views on the site.

4) Guest Posts

Find other blog sites that share your niche or common interest and post for them. Interact with their readers. This puts you in front of a larger audience giving you essentially free advertising (and hopefully these people will seek you out on your blog) and also improves search engine rankings.

Leave useful comments with a link in the URL section. The comment should be related to the article content itself. Capture people to your website by having a catchy bio line with SEO keywords and effective anchor text.

5) Avatar

People do business with those that they like, know and trust. The first way to establish that is by letting them see what you look like, whether it is a photograph (with eye contact) or a particular image that you would like to be associated with. Register with Gravatar to supply the photo or image.

The avatar can be a logo as well instead of a person. Keep in mind that it is an image that you will be using for a long time so choose wisely.

6) Drive Traffic to Your Site-Connect with Social Media

Tap into the power of the blogosphere. You can shave years off trying to get readers to your site, by referring your friends and connections on social media.

Social Media Bookmark Icon +

- **Facebook-** there are more people registered on this site than the population of many countries! Facebook enables you to interact on a general section, which is best left for friends, and establish a page, which can be used for business.

  Facebook pages can be customized with headers encompassing your company banner to further contribute to your branding. Include a call to action on the sidebar.

- **LinkedIn-** used for business connections as opposed to social interactions. This site enables you to join groups of like-minded people in addition to connecting with people.

  The catch is that you must know the people in advance or their email address, which you will be asked to repeat at the time a request for connection, is made.

- **Twitter-** comments are restricted to 140 characters or less. However, those 140 characters can be shortened urls that link back to posts where you can go into further depth on a topic.

  Unlike LinkedIn where you need permission from the second party to connect, on Twitter you can follow anyone (and see who else follows them). Find people in your niche and follow them as well as some of their followers. Out of reciprocity, some of these connections will follow you back.

- **YouTube-** allows users to upload their videos, view and share with others. Essentially, anyone can upload videos that everyone can see. Videos have been found to be the medium most virally distributed. Each one has embedded code placed by the owner of the video allowing others to seek them out or view their sites.

- **Pinterest-** enables users to share and manage images from interests and events. This website works with most smart phones, ipads and the major computer servers.

- **Stumbleupon-** finds and recommends online content to its consumers, enabling readers to rate photos, videos and the Web pages that have been referred based on their interests.

- **Digg-** supplies the most popular stories that are currently presented and talked about online. Clicking onto Digg lets you hone in on the best stories in your niche and the ones that your market is talking about while weeding out the millions of entries that appear on the Internet daily.

Chapter 21
Highlights

Starting To Blog: The 3 E's

Engage, Educate and Entertain. These are the 3 E's that any effective media should contain.

Blogging is no different. If your blog is interesting, educating and entertaining it will cause people to want to engage with you. Dare to be different and useful. Make sure however that you are in tune with your market.

Decide on what topics you want to blog about and develop a schedule or calendar with topics plotted out. It will get you in the habit of providing content regularly and your readers in the habit of expecting something from you.

Start with a memorable, attention-grabbing headline. Nothing attracts people to your blog like a catchy title.

Encourage readers to leave comments. Invite conversations and reactions to your posts.

The reward to having a successful blog is more engaging, personal content that grabs your audience's attention.

Chapter 22
Fast & Easy way to start your Blog Today!

1. Choose a title from your list.

So how do you know what title to use? Write about the one you have been thinking about the most. This topic should be the easiest for you to write about, as the words should just flow out of your fingers naturally and onto the keyboard.

The more emotion this topic evokes out of you the better. Don't worry about the wording of the title until after you are finished writing the content. Sometimes the perfect title can manifest itself after the body is completed.

2. Make a list with bullet points of all the things you want to talk about.

This is considered the fun part. Go crazy writing down anything you can think of that you want to talk about in this article. Turn these thoughts into short statements. The great thing is that it's easier to write articles like this as well, as it gives you structure.

3. Organize that list into headings and subheadings.

You will take notice that some of your bullet points will blend together. There may be 4 points that are all very similar so you can put them under one main thought. Some of these thoughts may not fit at all with the rest and you might find it will make a great topic for a whole other article.

4. Write as fast as you can and your mind will let you and worry about grammar and spelling later.

The more you tend to worry about spelling and grammar. the more you are stumping your creativity and imagination. Remember, the only reason someone wants to read your article is because it's entertaining and imaginative!

5. Jazz it up.

After you have gone through your article and corrected your grammar and spelling, you can add things like under- lining and bolding. This is quick and easy to do, but is much easier after you have written your article. Bolding a few key phrases also makes it easier to read and gives a reader a more enjoyable experience on your blog.

Chapter 23
Tips

10 Tips to make your Blog Stand Out

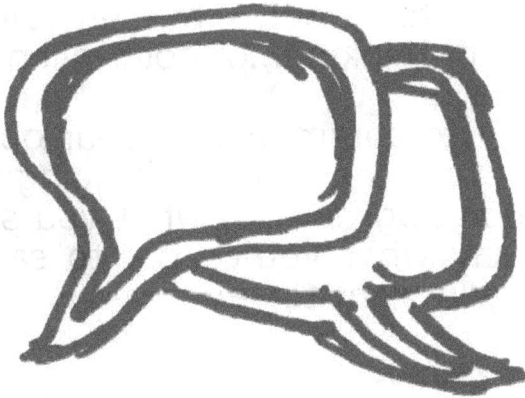

1. Make your opinion known

People like blogs - that's why they read them. They like blogs because people and not cor-porations write them. People want to know what other people think.

Yes, it sounds a bit out-there, but in this vir-tual age, where most communication between people happens online or via text/message and not in-person, one of the best ways you can get your message out virally besides writing and distributing an ezine, is through blogging.

So believe it or not, you are not the only per-son in the world who thinks the way you do. Blogging provides people all over the world an opportunity to belong – to gain validation for their way of thinking...of not feeling so alone.

It's a way to communicate your opinion in a safe environment – no one's going to hit you if they don't agree with what you say. So go ahead...say what you've got to say, exactly the way you want to say it.

2. Link like crazy.

Support your post with tons of links to other web pages that relate to your post.

3. Less is more

Make every word count. Give the maxi- mum amount of information with the least amount of words. However you say it, the bottom line is - time is finite and people are infinitely busy. Blast your knowledge into the reader at the speed of sound.

4. 500

400-500 words are the lengths that you should shoot for. Google and other search engines may not recognize your post if they are consistently too short. However, you can mix it up for personalization and have 250 word posts on occasion. Even some short humorous stories or quotes can make the occasional appearance to maintain your reader's interest.

5. Make Headlines snappy

Not only does this give you "ranking points" by search engines when you have your keywords within the headline, but it needs to grab the attention of your reader.

Studies show that 85% of your readers will never get beyond your title if it is boring. Instead, it will make it into the trash bin.

With so much entered on the web each day and a severe shortage of time to view it, everyone has gotten really adept at using the delete key!

6. Include bullet point lists

We all love lists. It structures the information in an easy format that allows us lazy people to skim the information and use what we need – no more, no less.

7. Make your posts easy to look over

Every few paragraphs insert a sub heading. Make sentences and head- lines short and to the point. Give the eyes a break and have a lot of white space so that scanners can easily peer over the post.

8. Consistency with your style

People like to know what to expect.

Once you have settled on a style for your audience, stick to it.

9. Edit, edit, edit

Before hitting the submit button, reread your post and cut out the stuff that you don't need.

Add in things you might want to add.

Then go ahead and fix all of those obvious grammar and spelling errors.

Then edit again. Proofread, proofread, and proofread. Read it out loud just to make sure.

THEN and ONLY then, hit submit.

Things to keep in Mind

➢ Encourage readers to leave comments. Invite conversations and reactions to your posts.

➢ Decide on what topics you want to blog about and develop a schedule or calendar with topics plotted out. It will get you in the habit of providing content regularly and your readers in the habit of expecting something from you.

➢ There are many different types and styles of blogs including written word blog to video blogging to photo blogging. Including multimedia in your blogs like videos and images can get the audience's attention, which is important in today's society of short attention spans.

Needless to say, one of the most important aspects of a blog is to make it interesting and create valuable content. Find out what makes your content valuable to your readers and target market and then give it to them!

Chapter 24
Review

Answer these questions to review what you've learned.

Questions:

- What is a blog?

- What are some ways to start your blogging career?

- Support your post with tons of _____ to other web pages that relate to your post.

- Start with a memorable, attention- grabbing _____.

- How do you figure out what title to use for your blog?

- True or False: Write as much as you can, the more the better. Explain your answer.

- Why do people have an interest in reading blogs?

- Why are people's comments and feedback so important for your blog?

- What is a keyword when writing a blog?

- What will making a list of bullet points help you with later on in your blog?

Chapter 25
What is an Ezine?

GET YOUR LATEST EZINE
NEWS & VIEWS ONLINE
(AND GET ON MY LIST)

An Ezine, short for Electronic magazine, typically shares similar features to blogs and online newspapers. It's sent out to a list of subscribers or potential clients that have raised their hand, expressing a desire to want it.

Typically an Ezine is distributed regularly - monthly, weekly or even daily, to various subscribers who have asked to receive it. Generally it is a very important tool for building an online business. It not only helps keep you in contact with your potential customers but it also allows you to help build a trusting and strong relationship with them. It also gives you a chance to build up your reputation while giving you another source of income.

Chapter 26
Why bother writing an Ezine?

Online shoppers spent in excess of $200 billion in 2011 and have been growing exponentially. Studies show that in 2012, money spent online actually surpassed shopping in brick and mortar stores. One of the best ways to convey your products and services online and attract some of those online dollars is with an ezine.

Benefits to having your own ezine

Exposure in ezines is one of the surest and most cost-effective ways to gain credibility and start building a relationship based on trust with your potential market – no matter what you're selling or promoting.

It goes a long way toward relationship building, which is crucial to the acquisition and retention of customers and clients.

By opting-in to receive your newsletters, subscribers have given you:

- Their information for your database

- Permission to send them promotions, announcements and ads from you

- An opportunity to promote your goods and services

- A vehicle for product launches

Ezines increase traffic to your website, a main advantage and goal to circulating the issue. Readers can then peruse your site and learn in greater depth about your products and services as well as what you are all about. Creating relevant information as well as content that has high quality, imparting helpful information, does this.

The more popular an ezine becomes, the more:

- Visitors and Sharers of your information come to the ezine

- Businesses and other websites will want to post ads on your ezine

- It becomes a source for solutions to problems people are struggling with

- Loyalty and trust of the subscribers

- You are viewed as an authority in the specific field

The greater the perception becomes that you are the authority and the higher your credibility, the greater the chances will be that people want to be associated with you by wanting your services or buying your products.

Personal Growth

Writing your own ezine also develops enhanced individual development. In essence, you are evolving as you continue to write.

Sure, you are writing about topics that you know about and reflect your business as well as those that are of interest to your target market. Yet, there will be topics where some research will be needed to keep up with new developments in the subject and the market. (And to answer questions that may arise from your subscribers) You are teaching and imparting new information to your readers while educating yourself.

Chapter 27
Starting Your Ezine

HOW DO I SET UP
MY EZINE?

Okay, you have decided that you want to get in on the action and start your ezine. The next thing you ask yourself is "How?"

Let's break this down by steps.

7 Steps to Start Your Ezine (From Conception to Pushing the Submit Button)

Step 1   Subject

The first thing that you want to establish is the topic of the ezine that reflects your website, goods and services. If you are in the vitamin supply business for example, you don't want the ezine to be all about knitting. This is an opportunity to let your business shine!

Ask yourself the following questions:

- What are clients asking when they call or email the company?

- What pains are felt in forums about the issues I will cover?

- What problems are discussed in chat rooms, relevant to my business that I can provide solutions to?

Compiling the answers to these questions will help formulate a plan as to what topics you will be covering and the ultimate subject of your publication.

Types of Content can be broken down into lists of tips, stories, technical instruction, case studies and new developments or breaking news in the field.

• Interview nationally or globally known figures and insert the interviews in with your content. In addition to providing useful information, association with these authorities will make you perceived as an authority as well.

Step 2   Naming Your Baby

Think of a name for your ezine. All newspapers and magazines have names and yours should have no exception. After all, you want people referring to it and this can't be done without a name.

Name selection is an art and not as easy as one might think. Don't be flippant or casual about naming your future "baby" as selecting the wrong name risks professional death- no readers, no subscribers.

Think of what people are searching for when they are looking for the type of information that

you will be providing. Incorporating these keywords into your title will let the name help work
to pro- mote itself as it rises to the top of Google
or other search engine pages. The name should
reflect the content and mission of your ezine.

- A great way to determine how well the name
  will be received is by getting the reaction of
  others. Usage of focus groups, utilized by larger
  concerns, can be costly. However, the same
  information can be obtained through surveys
  online. This can be done without cost through
  sites like:

- http://www.SurveyMonkey.com

- http://www.esurveyspro.com

- http://www.freeonlinesurveys.com

- http://www.kwiksurveys.com

Make sure that the name you have chosen can
be trademarked and a URL is available.

After all you don't want to slave over your issues
with writing and promotion, only to be promoting someone else or worse yet, receive a cease
and desist letter for all your hard work.

Step 3   Scheduling

Decide whether your ezine will be sent monthly,
biweekly, weekly, daily. The answer to the question of frequency will depend on your time and

commitment as well as the type of client or business you have.

One of the fastest ways to lose the readership that you amass is by disappointing them. If they expect your information to go out at a particular time or date and it is not forthcoming, they will no longer look for your ezine. So, whatever you have decided upon for scheduling, you must commit to this.

Would getting information from you irritate your client daily? Is there enough new information to send your ezine out frequently or is your field changing so frequently that a report sent out by you often is eagerly received? This must be balanced by having an interval that is too long (e.g. once or twice a year) where subscribers forget you or go elsewhere in search of the information that could have been provided by you.

Step 4   Choose the Theme, Look and Feel of the Ezine

Is there a color scheme in the company banner and logo? If so, this should be repeated in the ezine for consistency and recognition. The company banner and logo can also be prominently displayed on the ezine cover. It is showing that there is a connection.

Think of all the big companies you know. Whether it is Pepsi, Disney, IBM or others that come to mind, the logo and colors are consistent throughout anything that they distribute.

Looking at just the colors for some business brings instant recognition.

Let your readers into your life. Add a photo of yourself and staff. Subscribers can identify with people as well as banners, logos and colors.

Tell an interesting story where a problem presented itself and the outcome didn't go well at first. People love to see how others have fallen and yet been able to pick themselves up and learn a lesson to move forward.

Add case studies to illustrate how professional adversity was overcome to take the business from failure to success or how bankruptcy was turned around to racking in millions.

Step 5   Registration

Apply for an ISSN.

This stands for International Standard Serial Number, an eight-digit numeral identifying publications including digital serial publications. This series of numbers is used for identification and is linked to the title of the publication and type. Assignment is free. If the name changes, a new ISSN must be issued.

Serial Publications consist of issues sent out regularly with chronological or numerical order.

Is an ISSN necessary?

Whether this code is needed depends on the country from which the ezine originates. In some countries, all serial publications must have the ISSN and it is automatically assigned. The code must be printed on each issue.

In addition, EAN 13, the major bar- coding system for commercial distribution, uses the ISSN as the identifier. A bar code is created so that it can be catalogued for vendors if you will be selling the ezine. It is also used to catalogue the ezine in digital libraries.

It is possible to get the code prior to publishing the first issue of the ezine as long as information about the ezine is supplied accompanied by a sample issue or cover mock-up, editorial page designating the name and address of the publisher and masthead of the ezine.

The ISSN number assigned is for the ezine publication, not each issue; the code encompasses the whole publication, not individual issues. The only time a new code is assigned is if there is a change in title. However, having the code does not afford copyright protection.

Where is the Code visible?

The preferred site to print the code is in the upper right corner of the cover.

The eight- digit number should follow the letters ISSN. An alternative spot is the section where the copyright page sits or publisher information.

ISSN Vs. ISBN

This may be a confusing issue to the novice as they may be unknown acronyms. ISBNs are assigned to books and if there is more than one book in a series, each one must have its own number. On the other hand, ISSN, which is issued to serial publications, need only one code which encompasses the whole publication at large.

ISSN Availability

Yearly growth rate has been 60,000- 70,000 codes issued showing the growth of serial publications.

The Register is available online by the ISSN International Centre in Paris.

(See http://www.issn.org)

Step 6   Circulation

Select the distributor for the ezine. This will be the company or site that sends out your publication and archives it. There are many to choose from. Check out the list (which is not exclusive but most commonly used and a good jump off point to anyone's research into the selection:

- **AWeber** http://www.aweber.com

Advantages:

1. Very versatile with vast opportunity for personalization

2. Outstanding customer support

Disadvantages:

1. Subscriberlisthasacapof 25,000 people (which may seem like a lot when just starting out but larger companies have data bases much greater than this)

2. Plans are ore expensive than some other sites.

- **iContact http://www.icontact.com**

Advantages:

- Provides huge array of options for customization

- Integrates well with social media

Disadvantages:

1. Complex and Confusing for beginners

2. Huge number of options may not be used

- **ConstantContact**
http://www.constantcontact.com

Advantages:

1. Photo gallery available for ezine inserts

2. Greatsupportteam

Disadvantages:

- Works best on Firefox or Chrome Have interface problems with Safari

- Logo is at bottom of each newsletter

- **MailChimp http://www.mailchimp.com**

Advantages:

- Very easy to use for novices

- Free service tier which is great for starting out and developing a mail list

Disadvantages:

1. No phone support

2. Few options available

- **Campaign Monitor
  http://www.campaignmonitor.com**

Advantages:

1. Integrates with Google Analytics

2. Easy to use with Simple Dashboard

3. Reasonable price

Disadvantages:

- Features are difficult to use for the novice

- Analytical testing charges add up when used more frequently than offered by the plan.

- **Reach mail http://www.reachmail.com**

Advantages:

- Free plan available

- Loads of features to choose

- Excellent email and phone support

Disadvantages:

1. Not well known

- **InfusionSoft http://www.infusionsoft.com**

Advantages:

1. Has vast amount of features

2. Tutoring program (Infusionsoft University), which teaches how to use features and navigate system

Disadvantages:

1. Highly sophisticated system may not

   Be needed or used by novice

2. Expensive

Step 7   Cost

Many of the distribution sites give a free trial for 30-60 days before charging but it's amazing how fast time flies. In addition, for each added feature (e.g. archiving, photo gallery) adds up.

Line up sponsors to defray the cost of the ezine. Look for companies that can cross-market to your subscribers in a complementary business or those who could generate sales by using your same target market.

Chapter 28
Finding Content Easily

CANT THINK OF EZINE IDEAS?
USE YOUR BLOGS

One of the many objectives of your ezine is to get your subscribers to go to your website.

An easy way to get content and get your readers to click on the link to your website at the same time, is to place a portion of a blog post in the ezine itself with a link that asks the subscriber to click on the highlighted blue area often stating "click here to read more" where they will be taken to the remainder of the article.

Benefits of the blog referral technique include:

- Less time to write new information

- Reinforces information already given

- Teaches your subscriber to refer to your website where they can view products and services more extensively

- Allows your blog to do "double-duty"

Chapter 29
Marketing Successfully

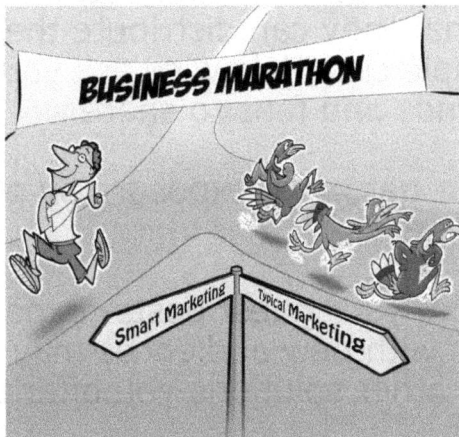

EZINES...
GREAT STRATEGY

1. Visibility

If you want people to opt-in to your ezine, you have to make your opt-in box easily visible. Place the sign-up box on:

- Every page of your website- visitors may not return to your home page when perusing your site. Don't make it a missed opportunity.

- All your social media sites- let your peers, like-minded people and fans know that you have an ezine for them to subscribe to.

- Share- ask friends and colleagues to share. Have a share button on the bottom of your ezine so that they can distribute the publication with a simple click. Likewise ask your social media friends and fans to share.

- Swap links- get more exposure by placing a link on other sites

- Bylines from your guest posts- exposure on other sites with new audiences may sign up to read what other solutions you offer them

Bylines from published articles- a great opportunity to capture subscribers by adding a catchy description of the ezine with a link to the subscription page.

- After your name on email responses- place an attention–getting depiction of the newsletter. As the email is spread around, so will chances for new subscribers.

- By lines on public forums or chat rooms- when you solve problems that people are struggling with; they want to read more about what you have to offer.

- Business cards –add link or QR code to ezine sign-up to let everyone know that the digital newsletter exists and is open for subscribing.

- Call to action-let people know to subscribe to your ezine from your blogs.

2. Increasing the Open Rate

The open rate is the percentage of sub- scribers who actually opened your ezine. Depending on which distribution company is used, more com- plete and specific analytics may be offered such as number of people that clicked onto the web- site from the ezine or how much time was spent viewing each page.

A rate of 30% is actually considered quite good. Especially since there is so much competi- tion out there now vying for attention.

4 Techniques to increase the Ezine open rate

Subject line- this is singularly the most impor- tant device and makes the difference between an open and never seeing the time of day. The subject line has to be catchy, and attention grab- bing to capture viewers but at the same time, be reflective of the content within the ezine issue. Make it less than 60 characters long.

From line- should identify you so that the viewer knows who sent it. This can be either the publisher's name or the name of the ezine itself depending on which way those subscribers most have a relationship with.

Wow them- make your content interest- ing and current, not "old hat" so that people will want to open the issue to find out what's new and how it pertains to them. The ezine further cements your relationship with clients and allows regular contact to keep in their minds.

Be Consistent- make the look and feel of the ezine the same with each issue. Like your logo, this ezine is further strengthening your brand-ing. Publish with regularity.

If you send out the ezine on the first of each month, then make a commitment to continue doing so. If you miss a few days, viewers will get out of the habit of looking for your information. However, research has shown that consumers don't want to receive the ezine more than twice in a month.

In other words, no commitment by you to your subscribers will translate into any commitment by your subscribers to you!

3. Scope Out Your Competition

Identify who your competitors are and sub-scribe to their ezines. See what their format is and how they approach the subject matter.

Cover the topics in a different way. Make sure to highlight your goods and services (which will help set you apart and why you are better...especially if you've gotten better ratings or reviews!)

Chapter 30
Sales Strategy

If the purpose of the ezine is to turn a profit other than promoting the goods and services on your website, there are 3 models to generate an income.

1. Affiliate Model

Advertise goods and services from business owners for which a relationship has been established. Commissions vary from 10% to 100% depending on the goal of the affiliation.

2. Subscription Model

Subscribers pay a regular fee to receive your valuable content. The recurring fee is billed and paid prior to receiving the information but the subscriber can opt-out at any time in most cases. (So stay interesting and valuable to them!)

3. Advertising Model

Sell advertising on the ezine. Rates depend on the prominence of the ad, frequency of appearance in the issues over the year and the size within the issue. Sponsorships, which garner more fees, would be prominently displayed in every issue over the course of a specified time (one year or several years)

Chapter 31
The Gift That Keeps Giving

YOU CANNOT AFFORD
TO STAND STILL

4 Long- term benefits of Ezines:

1. **Archives-** placing your ezines in storage, allows current and new subscribers to read old issues.

2. **Links-** More importantly, search engines and spiderbots will find an impressive number of links to your website. This contributes to a higher search ranking.

3. **Keywords-** With continued publication of news and content about the same category or niche, specific keywords will repetitively show up by search engines to your site and will identify you with these key- words. Then when others do an Internet search, you rise to the top in these fields.

4. **AdSense-** register with Google for AdSense so that certain ads appear on the ezines which generate money when viewers click on it.

Chapter 32
Be the Resource
Blast Out What's New

Let's face it. No one is the sole provider of breaking news. Just look at the television. There are 4-6 stations at any one time, trying to scoop each other and reporting on the same news. (Often news that social media has already tweeted out to their twibes up to a full day earlier!)

Provide resources promoting useful technology or services of others in your niche. Subscribers will appreciate it; competitors will love it!

What do you get out of this? Possibly you will get a reciprocal referral to your site. Definitely you get outgoing links back to your site, which is rewarded, on the ranking scale for search engines.

Chapter 33
Some Ezine Notes

Make your ezine an extension of your business.

Make a habit of saving useful things that you come across and place in folders on desktop or emails to easily find it for ideas about future articles or entries into the ezine. Wherever you store them, place it in an area where you can access them right away.

In order to have an effective Ezine:

- **Keep it clean!** – Have a clean design. Keep it neat and easy to read. Don't jumble it up with a lot of different decorations.

- **Good content** – Make sure to give your subscribers information they find helpful and can ACTUALLY use.

- **Original** – write some articles yourself and give your subscribers something they can't get anywhere else. A valuable tip you learned in your vast experience, an inspiring story, something – a piece of yourself that's original and true.

- **Personality** – Go ahead and add a little of YOU into your ezine while making it a little fun and personal.

- **Reliability** – If your ezine comes out on Thursday, make sure you send it out every Thursday. If you can't for whatever reason, make sure to let your subscribers know ahead of time! Subscribers need reliability. They are not interested in flakes.

- **Knowledge** – make sure your business and your ezine deal with something you know about and are also very passionate about.

- **Scripts aren't just for actors...**

  Study other people's ezines and base your template on one you find to be most appealing to your target subscribers.

Chapter 34
Key Points

> An Ezine is simply just an online magazine that typically shares similar features with a blog and also with online newspapers, it's easiest to think of it as a magazine or a newsletter that is just published online.

> A great reason as to why Ezines are such an acceptable way of building and publishing an online business is because it is a perfect opportunity for many different people to be able to work from home.

- ➢ Follow the 4-step method!

- ➢ 6 ways to publishing a good ezine:

    1. Keep it clean!

    2. Good content

    3. Originality

    4. Make it personal

    5. Reliability

    6. Knowledge

- ➢ Go ahead and add a little of YOU into your ezine while making it a little fun and personal.

- ➢ At all costs avoid rambling on and leave out all those boring details that aren't crucial to what you learned.

- ➢ Leverage your blog posts and article publications

- ➢ Leverage participation in forums, chat rooms and guest blogs

Chapter 35
Review

Answer these questions to review what you've learned.

1. What is an Ezine?

2. Through an ezine you're able to keep your customers informed of any and all new _____ and or _____ on your site.

3. What does the 4-step method consist of?

4. What are 3 things you need in order to publish a good ezine?

5. It is essential to make sure that there are no careless and or simple mistakes in your ezine such as _____ and _____.

6. Why are ezines such an acceptable way of building and publishing an online business?

7. What is the main goal that you want to achieve with your ezine?

8. Why would you want to imagine talking to a good friend or family member when writing your ezine?

9. True or False: It's a bad idea to add any personal information to your ezine. Explain your answer.

10. Why would you add some of your own articles into your ezine?

Chapter 36
What is a Newsletter?

A newsletter, which serves as a vehicle to communicate with a group of like- minded people, is a publication to spread news. When written well, newsletters are impressive content marketing tools.

Many small businesses write newsletters as part of their marketing strategy to help promote their own products and or services as well as helping to strengthen internal communication within the organization.

If written well, newsletters can help create stronger relationship with custom- ers, suppli- ers, and employees, all while contributing toward the overall success of the business.

*Though most information is sent digi- tally, the data can be deleted with one stroke and never be read. A newsletter, sitting on a desk top in full view may get people to pick it up and read.

Chapter 37
Benefits

Why distribute a newsletter?

Newsletters usually serve more than one purpose. Before making a commitment to write and distribute a newsletter, have a mission or purpose for taking this action.

Some typical reasons that companies and organizations distribute newsletters are listed below:

1. Motivational Tool

   a. Newsletters can be used to recognize top performers in a company. This builds employee morale, and encourages others to perform as well or better – to get the recognition.

b. Newsletters can also be used to spotlight certain events – either in the past, or upcoming ones.

c. As a motivational tool in an organization, newsletters can result in inter-departmental relationship- building, it can increase sales, and also build a camaraderie between employees that shows that they are part of a community – not just a bunch of people stuck working in the same place at the same time.

2. Solicitation Tool

a. Many organizations such as schools and churches use newsletters as a means to ask for help. Whether the help comes in the form of volunteering time, donating money or items, attendance to an event, or feedback about a particular decision made by the organization, the point is to get as many members to help make the organization more effective and efficient.

3. Information Tool

a. Some organizations also use newsletters to publish information about certain accomplishments, goals, benchmarks, upcoming changes to the organization, industry and market trends, or social events.

4. Educational Tool

   a. This form of use is similar to using a newsletter as an informational tool – with the added focus on taking action toward a goal, or the resulting outcome of an event.

   b. For instance, a newsletter can be used to share tips and ideas – like recipe sharing or cleaning tips. It can also be used to announce certain changes in procedure or how to learn a new skill.

   c. As an educational tool, a newsletter must have information that teaches something new to the reader.

5. Marketing Tool

   a. As a marketing tool, organizations publish newsletters to promote and sell their products and services, to build awareness about their products, create and develop brand recognition, and as a way to reach out to the target market.

6. Communication Tool

   a. A newsletter is a communication tool – that's the bottom line. It keeps your name and business in the mind of your market and further strengthens your branding.

Chapter 38
Are Newsletters SPAM?

Whenever people see the term "email market-ing", they automatically think of email promo-tions- as in scenarios when you buy a product and decide to check the little box that says the "send me periodic mailings with news of related products and services.

This is used as permission to bombard your email inbox with sales letters and promotions on an all too frequent basis.

That's SPAM – unsolicited emails.

Although newsletters fall into the email- mar-keting category, they are not considered SPAM.

Why?

In order to receive a newsletter, you must sub-scribe to one by volunteering your email address and name (at the very least). This signifies an interest to read the content of the newsletter

All contact information of subscribers must be stored in a secure database to avoid access to hackers.

Another distinguishing factor of newsletters from SPAM is that once you don't find them interesting anymore, or the novelty of it wears off, you can opt out of your subscription by clicking on a link at the end of the publication.

Email Promos vs. Newsletters

If newsletters are a method of promoting a company's products via electronic media, how is this different from email promotions?

Email promotions specifically seek out to get immediate action.

The keyword here is **immediate.**

In general, promotional emails are pretty short-term unless for some reason it is part of a sequenced campaign. In return, if the recipient doesn't respond more or less immediately to the offer, then chances are that the value of the email is generally lost.

This is where newsletters come into play. Newsletters are about being able to build long-term relationships. Their basic and primary goal is to help strengthen the relationship between the consumer or prospect and the publishing entity.

The overall objective is usually to help induce actions long-term.

Newsletters aim toward making the recipient of a newsletter much more likely at some time in the future to go about the kind of actions that are most ultimately desired by you, the pub-lisher, and then taking them again and again if it's possible.

To sum this all up, newsletters help build long-term impact and influence on your relationship between you and your customers.

Chapter 39
Preparation

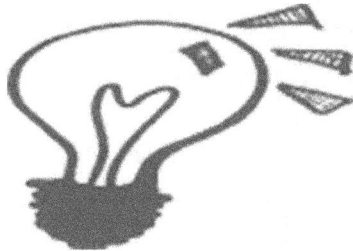

Before starting your newsletter, there are several considerations to decide upon in preparation of writing the newsletter in order to be successful.

Steps:

1. Setting the Goal

Figure out the goal you wish to achieve through the newsletter.

Common goals include:

- Lead generation to your website or business

- To showcase products and services

- Educate on the latest technology or how products work

- Inform readers on breaking news

- To generate revenue

- For entertainment or fun

2. **Map out the content** Define the subjects that will be covered and how specific or general the content will be based on the goal set in step 1.

3. **Picture your reader** Know your target market. The style, vocabulary, nuance and slang phrases will all be dependent on which the news- letter is written for. Describe your market's:

- Gender

- Age range

- Education

- Career

- Ethnic background

- Economic status

- Social Status

- Geographical location

- Handicaps or challenges

4. Delivery frequency and mode

Determine how often the newsletter will be issued

- Monthly

- Weekly

- Daily

- Biweekly

Decide on mode of delivery.

- Digitally

- Postal Service In House Mailroom delivery Placement at public site (e.g. supermarket)

5. Staff and length of newsletter

To some extent, the amount of staff required to write, edit and publish the newsletter will be dependent on the scope of the project. How large is the newsletter? (2 pages, 20 pages with photographs) If just starting out, the staff may consist of one person, which grows over time.

6. Features

Decide on the sections to be featured. Dividing the newsletter into sections will help with content organization.

Divisions can include:

- Advice column

- Letters to the editor

- Event calendars

- Interesting helpful articles

Helpful tips

7. Software

Layout programs can aid in making the news-letter appear professional.

Programs that offer easy to use and good layout include:

- Adobe InDesign

- Quark

- Microsoft Word

Chapter 40
How to Write a Newsletter

There are many newsletter templates available online. Before you download a selection, look over the following check- list and determine what format you want to present the actual newsletter to your readers.

1. Organize your thoughts. Prioritize the topics or subjects. Most newsletters actually feature the larger or more important articles on the very first few pages and then place the smaller and less important ones towards the back.

2. Be mindful of deadlines! If any material is time sensitive, make sure it is included in an

issue that allows delivery to readers in a timely manner.

3. Match the tone of the newsletter with the target audience. A business or corporate newsletter will be more formal whereas one for teens may be friendlier with less of a structured attitude.

4. Take your audience into consideration. Make sure that every article you include in your newsletter is aimed toward the group of people you are trying to reach. Ask yourself this: Does this article benefit or inform the reader receiving the newsletter?

5. Overall and most importantly, keep it simple. A newsletter is meant to be very informative and also straightforward. Make sure to cleanly and clearly relate all of the important information and facts before you decide to focus in on the less important articles that also receive less attention.

6. Turn in your newsletter on time. If this is going to be a regularly published newsletter your readers expect to be able to read it on a regular basis!

If you fail to deliver a complete newsletter on time it makes it seem like you are a unreliable news source and will most likely turn some if not most of your readers away while the few that you have left will not have any confidence in your publication

7. Make sure that any writers that help contribute to your newsletters are clearly aware of all deadlines, goals and importantly, restrictions.

8. Start to pay attention to any feedback that you receive in regards to your newsletter. Make sure to note both positive and negative attitudes directed towards your publication it would help determine your demands and whether or not you are meeting those needs.

9. Figure out the ROI (return on investment of the Newsletter. What are the costs, the subscriber number, the amount that ads and sponsors bring in and any other expenses or revenue? Make a chart.

Chapter 41
Electronic Newsletters Vs. Hardcopy

Most newsletters are published on websites or distributed digitally to cut down on costs in this tough economy.

However, people like printed newsletters to handle manually and read while on trains or forced to wait in situations where they are spending time in any given areas like waiting rooms. Remember, the prime objective of a newsletter is to promote interaction with the client and the newsletter distributor.

If you can continually encourage the client to interact with a business through a news- letter, there is a better chance that there will be client retention.

Hardcopy

Studies show that those who have physical newsletters, read them more thoroughly as opposed to having a digital copy with an all-to-easy option of hitting the delete key.

Then too, when the newsletters are in hard-copy form, they can put it on their desk for later with colleagues getting a glimpse of it as they go by. (Becoming subscribers as well)

Tips

Here are some tips for launching these news-letters...and getting throngs of subscribers.

First, we need to make a few assump- tions. Let's just say that you already have a website. This website is promoting your writing services. You want to further mar- ket your services via newsletter so you can keep your finger on the pulse of your market.

One way to do this is to offer a free newsletter subscription. But first, you need to entice your readers to read your newsletter and subscribe. With all the SPAM being distributed, people are wary of subscribing to just anything.

You need to offer something interesting, com-pelling, and something that fulfills an un-met need in the market.

Be it tips on how to become a writer, how to find the right writer for your job, or how much to charge for typical writing jobs – make the content of your newsletter interesting to your readers.

You can also attract subscribers by offering a free gift with subscription. A short eBook on a topic that your readers will find helpful is a great way to get people to sub- scribe to your newsletter.

Chapter 42
How Do I Get People to Subscribe?

Your biggest fans are subscribers. They've raised their hands and stated enthusiastically that they actually want to hear what you have to say; they want you to contact them.

More importantly, they are eager to interact and engage, purchasing the products and services that you highlight. What's more, avid subscribers will pass the coupons and deals on to friends and families, increasing the subscription base and sale of services.

So how do you get these avid fans?

The Secret to Capturing Subscribers

1) Opt-in Box

The opt-in box leading to the enrollment form for the newsletter needs to be prominently displayed on your website. If website navigation is difficult and the opt- in box can't be found, potential subscribers will not take the additional time and effort looking for it!

Studies show that most visitors only see the first half of a website and don't scroll down so having the opt-in box on top in- stead of the bottom of a webpage can triple those signing up for the newsletter.

You have to make your opt-in box easily visible. Place the sign-up box on:

- Every page of your website- visitors may not return to your home page when perusing your site. Don't make it a missed opportunity.

- All your social media sites- let your peers, like-minded people and fans know that you have a newsletter for them to subscribe to.

- Share- ask your social media friends and fans to share.

- Swap links- get more exposure by placing a link or ad on other sites

- Bylines from your guest posts- exposure on other sites with new audiences may sign up to read what other solutions you offer them

- Bylines from published articles- a great opportunity to capture subscribers by adding a catchy description of the newsletter with a link to the subscription page.

- After your name on email responses- place an attention–getting depiction of the newsletter. As the email is spread around, so will chances for new subscribers be disseminated.

- Bylines on public forums or chat rooms- when you solve problems that people are struggling with; they want to read more about what you have to offer.

- Business cards- add link or QR code to the newsletter sign-up to let everyone know that the newsletter exists and is open for subscribing.

Call to action-let people know to subscribe to your newsletter from your blogs.

2) Social Media

Produce an attention-grabbing icon for the newsletter, which links to the news- letter's enrollment form. Place this link on the front of your Facebook Page in a prominent location.

As each new issue of the newsletter is published, create a synopsis with a re- minder on the various social media sites, LinkedIn, Twitter, and Facebook. Ask people on your social media sites to sign up for the newsletter.

3) Have I got something for you!

Offer a discount or special deal for your products and services that only subscribers are eligible for. This should be done sporadically so as not to dissuade routine business until offers and sales are initiated.

Place valuable coupons in the newsletter.

Offer special videos podcast or discs to first-time subscribers.

4) Signature

Insert the newsletter name and link after your email signature and have it appear consistently, whenever your name appears.

5) Upsell Thank you

Whenever a client or customer purchases a product, ask them to subscribe to your newsletter in the body of the thank you page. Remember to capture the name and the email at the time of the purchase so that you can send them information about new products in the future.

Here, you can also mention that YOU are enrolling them for the newsletter and they can unsubscribe if they want to. This however, can be a little tricky because there will be some room for doubt then as to whether everyone on the newsletter list really wants to be there.

There is a segment of the population who are "tire-kickers". They want to see what you have to offer but they are not ready to buy.

Capture names of people with email addresses, who have perused the product sites, even if a purchase was not made. They may be back later but you don't want to lose the opportunity of contacting them in the future. Stressing a free gift or discount to this segment will sometimes be enough to tip the scales over onto signing up.

6) Talk about the newsletter

Promote your newsletter to audiences when you attend seminars or give talks and let them know what benefits they can receive by signing up. Have some hand- outs or samples of the newsletter with you and a subscription link or QR code for them to access the enrollment form.

7) Showcase the newsletter in your 30-second presentation

Mention the newsletter in your "elevator speech" at meetings when everyone goes around the room presenting themselves. Invite the attendees to visit your website and sign up for the newsletter.

8) Display testimonials

Let perspective subscribers know what your raving fans have to say about you and have complimentary they are! Place this adjacent to the opt-in box after you have gotten permission to do so. Even more powerful is having the testimonials in video format on the website.

9) Publish articles

Write pertinent articles and publish them every-one- online, other people's sites, and in trade-shows with a mention of the newsletter and link to it on your resource box.

10) Use Friends as Resources

Encourage friends and peers to promote your newsletter to their "herd" or mailing lists. Offer to swap information from your friends to your list in exchange.

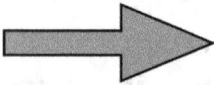

Keep Your list fresh! People's data changes or they may opt out. Continually promote the newsletter to grow the database list.

Chapter 43
Tips & Tricks

Newsletters are considered to be one of the most important communication tools used in any organization – for profit or nonprofit. Usually businesses use news- letters to help increase sales.

One of the main purposes of writing and or marketing a newsletter is to actually GET sub- scribers and then turn them around into buyers.

There are two very essential factors that should be kept in mind when it comes to writing a business newsletter:

1. Content

2. Design

Most newsletters that are actually considered "good" contain a featured article, news updates,

regular columns, employee profiles, and advertisement and feedback sections.

The Featured article:

This is the most important part of your entire
newsletter. It really should be overly informative and interesting while urging your readers to
read even more and take action such as making
an online purchase.

The News section:

The news section of your newsletter can actually highlight any upcoming events or basic news
about your industry that will somehow appeal to
your readers.

The Regular column section:

Specifically go about and include articles that
will help emphasize on accomplishments and
success stories in this section, but make sure to
keep them short and precise.

   Also remember that less is more. Each of your
articles should complement the other in able to
reach your goal hence turn your subscribers into
buyers.

Including success stories:

Take a basic employee profile information and
highlight their achievements. As an example,
you could write something like: "Paul has been

Company X's marketing manager for the last 12 years.

During this time, he has been involved in the implementation of many successful marketing campaigns and has been a treasured member of the company. Thank you, Paul, for your dedication and loyalty. We wouldn't be here without your hard work." Trust me - people enjoy reading success stories no matter where it is they happen.

Special things to keep readers interested:

Remember this...rewards can bring rewards. Any type of prize-winning competitions that you include will pull more readers in and start subscribing to your newsletter.

Get your feedback!

Get feedback and use it to your advantage, include various feedback sections in your newsletters at the very end so that you know what is working and what simply isn't and if your readership is strong or not.

Chapter 44
Key Concepts

> Newsletters are considered to be one of the most important communication tools used whether you're running a business or even a nonprofit organization.

> Whether good or bad, pay attention to any feedback that you receive in regards to your newsletter.

Keep it simple, a newsletter is meant to be very informative and also straightforward.

➢ Specifically go about and include articles that will help emphasize on accomplishments and success stories in the regular column section.

➢ Organize your thoughts!!!

➢ If you fail to deliver a complete newsletter on time it makes it seem like you are an unreliable news source.

➢ A newsletter is a piece of information; therefore make sure that every article you include in your newsletter is aimed toward the group of people you are trying to reach.

➢ Newsletters basic and primary goal is to help strengthen the relationship between the consumer or prospect and the publishing entity.

➢ Encourage interaction. Have a section within the newsletter where people can exchange their thoughts and reactions (as in letters to the editor)

➢ Have a human-interest story that illustrates a point that is being made.

Stories add to strengthen connection and relationships.

➢ Insert some light humor, comic or comic relief. It is a break from all the serious information. People love to laugh.

➢ Newsletters aim toward making the recipient of a newsletter much more likely at some time in the future to go about the kind of actions that are most ultimately desired by you, the publisher, and then taking them again and again if it's possible.

Chapter 45
Review

See how much you've learned by answering the questions

Questions:

1. What is a newsletter?

2. What is the main purpose of a newsletter?

3. What is a good question to ask yourself when taking your audience into mind?

4. Is it important to keep all feedback in mind, good and bad? Why?

5. If you fail to turn in a newsletter on time why would this make you look like an unreliable source?

6. A newsletter is meant to be very _____ and _____.

7. True or False, A newsletter should be incredibly difficult to understand while still being informative. Explain your answer

8. What is the very first step to writing a newsletter?

9. Make sure that any writers that help contribute to your newsletters are clearly aware of all _____, _____ and importantly, _____. What is the main difference between an email promotion and a newsletter?

Chapter 46
White Papers

A Rose By Any Other Name

Depending on the niche, many clients or customers are unfamiliar with what a white paper actually is. In many markets, a white paper is also referred to as:

Depending on the niche, many clients or customers are unfamiliar with what a white paper actually is. In many markets, a white paper is also referred to as:

- Free Report

- Free Book

- Guide

- Handout

- Briefing

- Bulletin

- Guidebook

- Position paper

- Release

- Biased brochures

Thus it is important when discussing a white paper with perspective clients that one is mindful of other synonyms that the client may be better acquainted with.

What is a white paper?

To put it best, a white paper is a documented report that helps present a problem or situation, and offers to solve it with a possible solution.

Typically, a white paper is used to argue a specific point or explanation to a problem.

Even though white papers originated in government policy, they have become a pretty common way to help introduce technology along with different products.

The publication of a white paper is in order to test the waters of the public's opinion in regards to a controversial policy while helping to enable the government.

For commercial use, white papers refer to documents that are used by businesses as sales or marketing tools.

Originally the term "white paper" branched off from the term "white book", which is just another way of saying an official government publication.

Government White Papers

White papers are distributed by our government and help to organize policy on a current topic of concern. Even though a white paper may be an advisement to stand for details of a new legislation, it does show a clear drive on the part of a government to help pass a new law.

Local, state, and national governments use white papers as a method to analyze specific situations. The analysis presented in the white papers is then used as de- cision-making tools to better serve the citizens of the area where the situation exists.

Sometimes the issue might concern the budget - how to better utilize the moneys in order to maximize the benefit it brings to the people. Other times, a white pa- per might be used to analyze the pros and cons of building a structure that benefits a segment of the popula- tion and how this, in turn, benefits everyone.

For instance, if a city was debating whether or not to build a Senior Center - a building that senior citizens of the city can utilize for senior- related events and gath- erings - in a park that is currently being used as a baseball field for a local com- petitive Little League team, a white paper supporting the construction of the Senior Center could discuss the benefits that the build- ing of the Senior Center would bring to the city.

On the other hand, a white paper that was pro Little League could also be writ- ten, listing all the benefits of keeping the park as-is, and analyzing all the revenue brought in by the Little League games played in the park.

Each white paper discusses the positive - the benefits of each specific argument. The citizens and decision-makers involved can base their decision on the analysis presented in the white paper.

Governments as decision- making tools for years have used white papers. Today, many businesses use white papers as well.

Commercial white papers

Starting in the early 1990s the word white paper started to refer to other documents that were used by businesses as marketing tools. White papers like this try to argue that certain benefits of specific technologies, policies, or products that are for solving a specific problem.

For instance, if you were a manufacturer of cell phones, and your company is in the process of launching an updated version of the original model, it would behoove you to publish a white paper describing the new product, its differences from the old one, and how these updates benefits your customers in their daily lives.

Typically, the language in a white paper is a mixture of techno-speak and marketing buzzwords. It might sound simple, and if it does, perhaps this is the perfect niche for you. However, for many writers, finding the perfect balance between technical talk and marketing language can be quite challenging.

As a writer, you must know the product intimately. It is vital to the credibility of your client - and their bottom line - to be able to explain in detail what each update does, the nuances of the technology, and how the technology can be applied by the user to his or her daily life in order to improve it somehow.

Chapter 47
White Paper Applications

White papers typically have 4 commercial applications:

1. Business benefits:

Presents and defends a company's decision to develop or utilize a particular technology.

Examples:

- Company A is updating their telephone technology from a human operator to an automated one.

- The whitepaper highlights the need to change in order to expedite service by simply pressing a button when listening to the help menu offered by the automated operator.

- The whitepaper also discusses the benefits of switching to an automated service to the user in terms of saving money. Because the company is saving money by automating this particular service, that savings is then passed on to the customer.

- Most commonly used whitepaper marketing type because it is the perfect combination of technical feature explanation and business benefit highlights.

- This whitepaper type is written to speak to a specific market. It emphasizes a particular problem experienced by that market, and how a certain feature of the product can solve that problem.

2. Technical Benefits:

Helps to describe how a certain technology may work.

- People don't like change. The white paper points out the barriers to acceptance of the new technology and how it overcomes the objections.

- Explains how new features work and the benefits that they provide.

3. Hybrid:

Discusses the technical details of a product and lists the benefits of each feature in one concise document.

- Combination of both business benefits white paper and technical white paper.

- The white paper explains why a decision was made, and how the change resulted in an increase in cash flow, thus making it possible to add more programs that benefit the children's education.

4. Policy:

Argues for a specific political solution to an existing economic challenge experienced by the target market.

This type of white paper explains in a positive light why a particular decision was made that affected the way a company or organization functions. It attempts to solve a dilemma or crisis currently experienced by the target audience of the organization.

For instance, school district A decides to reorganize the chain of command structure as well as the salary structure of administrators.

Chapter 48
Benefits of a White Paper
(aka White Book)

BOOKS CAN BE DANGEROUS.
THE BEST ONES SHOULD BE
LABELED "THIS COULD
CHANGE YOUR LIFE."
                    —HELEN EXLEY

The effects of publishing white papers for a business can be quite dramatic.

5 Great Benefits of White Papers include:

1. Validation

Studies show that published white papers are one of the best tools for validating credibility, ethics and reliability of a company and usefulness of its products

Written by a credible third-party source, it also validates the business, goods and services in a powerful way.

2. Designation

Corroborates the business position as a thought leader and the white paper illustrates how this is so. White papers highlight the solutions by telling stories supporting company solutions, promoting your brand.

3. Lead Generation

Revenue growth increases dramatically with the rise of leads and conversions of leads to sales by:

- Demonstrating visionary skills

- Showcasing effective analytical skills

- Enhancing strategic claims

4. Promotion

Takes the business, solutions and brand to a higher level.

5. Competitive Edge

Fortifies a company's position against the competitors while highlighting how the company overcame challenges to arrive at the most effective solutions.

Objectives can be simply stated as aiming to:

- Demonstrate authority or thought leadership

- A Generate sale leads

- Conversion of leads to buyers and consumers

Chapter 49
Preparation

**IDEA DAYS ARE
PROFIT DAYS!**

Before rushing to construct the white paper, preparation is involved. Sure, write down all the ideas that are rushing through your mind and then take the following actionable steps.

14 Actions for Success

1. Meet with the Client and the significant decision-makers. Discuss their goals and the deadline for the assignment

2. Discuss the objective for the paper- what does the client want to highlight and accomplish? What new and key information does the client want to present?

3. Pinpoint the topic for the paper and the angle.

4. Identify the problem and the pain points that the market is struggling with

5. Ascertain the solutions to the problem and why it is the solution

6. Identify the target market. Who is the reader that the paper is aimed at? (Age, gender, occupation, economic status, geographical location, etc.) Know all about the readers and what makes them tick.

   This is a crucial step because it is vital to write the white paper in a way that will catch your reader's attention and hold it for the duration of the paper's discussion.

   You need to speak the target reader's language, be familiar with their issues, and pose a solution that will present itself in such a way that it convinces the reader that it is the best possible solution for them.

7. Ascertain the experts. Who devised the product? Who provides the services? Who invented the technology?

   Interviewing the right people is imperative. Key subjects include those most knowledgeable about the product, those involved in the decision-making process, and those most affected by the decisions.

   Present these interviews as evidence in support of the proposed solution. Interviewing the right people is imperative. Key subjects include those most knowledgeable about the product, those involved in the decision-making process, and those most affected by the decisions.

   Present these interviews as evidence in support of the proposed solution.

   Find out if the client has a list of testimonials that can be used. If not, find out if there are some happy customers that would be willing to answer interview questions on the record. Interviews are used to reinforce the solution to the issue addressed in the white paper.

8. Interviewing customers about their insights will help you assemble a stronger case, thus making the white paper more effective in its goal to ultimately boost your client's bottom line

9. Gather printed material for the product or service that the white paper will be discussing.

Get the instruction manuals, training guides, stock briefs, brochures and history of the product, services or company.

Gather as many documents as possible. You can always pare down the amount of data you will use in the white paper. It's more difficult to defend a position with a lack of information than it is to have more than enough information and select which documents you want to use to your advantage.

10. Arrange times to interview the key experts and clients from #7 and #8.

11. Draft the outline.

12. Present the outline with the ideal responses for the goal, readers, and objectives to the Client and decision- makers for approval.

13. Make any adjustments based on their responses and submit for their approval again.

14. You're now ready! Write the White Paper

Chapter 50
Writing a White Paper

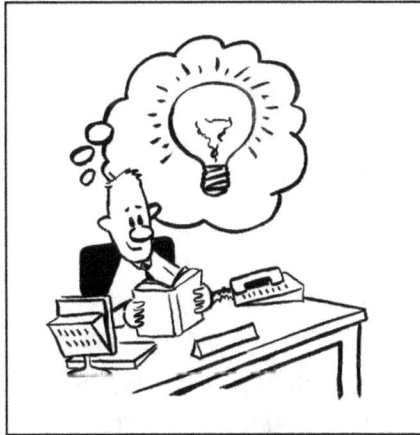

WHITE PAPERS:
PROBLEMS & SOLUTIONS

Two approaches

Basically, you can approach writing a white paper in one of two ways.

1. Focus on self-interest or the interests of the organization.

   - This approach concentrates on featuring the product and explaining the benefits - a formulaic one-two style.

   - More often than not, this white paper will not be read by your intended audience because it is dry, boring, and reads more like a brochure pushing a product than an analysis of why purchasing this thing benefits the reader.

   - An example would be, "This White Paper Introduces Company A's New Gadget That Does Cool Stuff"

   - There is no WIIFM in this document - What's In It For Me. The reader is not compelled to read this type of white paper because although it explains the benefits (some of us can argue that doing cool stuff could be construed as a benefit), it does not highlight or address the interest of the reader. It does not talk about a problem the reader could be experiencing and how the product can solve it.

2. Concentrate on the interests of the audience.

   a. This approach is more successful because it is written to address a specific problem that the reader is experiencing, and describing how the product can be used to solve that problem.

   b. For example, "This White Paper Discusses How A Phone App Can Help You Find A Freight Service Company That Best Fits Your Shipping Needs"

   c. This white paper is more likely to be read by someone who is looking to expedite the shipping process of his or her organization and perhaps save money in the process. It addresses - right away - the WIIFM principle.

Chapter 51
The Backbone

There is a typical structure by which a white paper is composed.

There are 9 various sections, which are as follows:

1. Title

Write a compelling headline, which grabs the attention of the target market. This headline needs to be benefit driven, not feature oriented. Having numbers in the title that proves a point strengthens the title.

2. Executive Summary or Abstract

Capture the reader with direct statements and a summary of what the paper deals with which will be proven later on.

3. Introduction

Define the issue and delineate the his- tory of the problem or situation from the beginning until the current time. Illustrate the issue in a way that your target market shares.

4. Problem defined

Pinpoint the problem that your company or product solves and present it in great detail from the pain points that your clients are experiencing.

5. Stated solution

Educate readers as to the current state of technology and what is going on in your niche now related to the defined problem, how competitors are handling the situation and how your solution is the answer to the prob- lem that the viewers are struggling with. Use charts, graphics, tables and statistics to sup- port your claims. Citing industry experts and authorities, sprinkling in their quotes to bol- ster your argument is very helpful.

6. Solution in depth

In this section, all the evidence proving how fantastic your solution is gets inserted. The quotes that have been gathered and testimo- nials are placed here and the solution is now delineated in great depth.

In addition to the claims put forth, also compare your solution to the competitors, highlighting why your product or service is much better. Case studies that confirm your claims can be used here as well.

7. Benefits

This section is the heart of the paper where it takes hold of the reader and gives lots of guarantees that your solution will be the answer to their prayers. Values to add here include an increase of ROI (return on investment), application speed and quality assurances.

8. Summary

Write this section as a standalone piece as many readers; scanning the white paper will only view this part. Stress all the benefits that your solution provides. Let the readers know all the risks and sacrifices they expose themselves to by not utilizing your goods or services.

It is important to strongly highlight all the main selling points and advantages that your solution provides and end with the most crucial selling point that you want to drive home and have remembered.

9. Call to action

In terms of leveraging the paper, this is actually the most important section as it is telling the reader, what you would like them to do.

While it's nice that you are educating your readers, you also want to take the time and money you invested toward creating and disseminating the white paper, and have it go to a particular action.

Examples of actions are:

- Sign up for a free consultation

- Opt-in for a blog or ezine

- Get a free trial

- Get a coupon

Basically, you want to capture the name, email and a little information about them which signing up for your calls to action will achieve.

Chapter 52
Format and Outline

Formatting Your White Paper

There really is no specific length that your white paper should be but anything from five to twenty pages long should be sufficient. Just keeps in mind that having anything longer than that and you might start to lose you reader's attention.

Your white paper should be separated into smaller sections with easy to read titles. Think about it, whenever you read something you're not sure you are interested in don't you usually skim over the material first? Why would your readers be any different?

Most white papers won't be read from front to back. Instead, they will be just looked over for the information that the reader finds most important or applicable to his or her situation.

4 Steps to Creating Your White Paper Outline

Different outlines for white papers vary depending on the content. However, if you follow these basic steps, you're sure to have the foundation for a well-organized and well-written white paper.

1. General Overview

- Introduce the problem being experienced by the reader, and the solution proposed by your client.

- Briefly state your case and how it works to solve the current issue faced by your target audience.

2. Key Points

a. Support your case by listing facts and figures to help back up the statements made in the general overview.

b. The more support, the better.

c. This is where you, as a writer, explain the technology in great detail, highlighting each feature and listing how every feature provides an irrefutable and irresistible benefit to the target market.

3. Use Examples

a. This is the section where you insert interviews and real life applications of the technology, as a solution to whatever issue is in question.

b. You can't have too many examples to help the reader visualize how the particular solution proposed is the best possible solution.

4. Summary

a. Just like it sounds. Re-emphasize your initial line of reasoning and bring it all together into one neat little package.

b. Reiterate some examples and real life applications of the solution and use those points to defend the proposed solution and illustrate how the recommended resolution is the best possible choice for everyone involved.

Hints & Tips

Here are some things to keep your eye on the ball as you write your white paper:

1. Stick to the point!

a. As writers and public speakers, we do this a lot - and we encounter it often in our personal lives as well. Staying focused on a topic is not the easiest thing to do.

b. The best way to avoid going off on a tangent - which is easy to do when discussing a technical topic - is to write it down right away.

c. When writing, it is also a good idea to proofread and edit as you go along - to ensure that - if you go off topic - that you can bring the discussion back on topic before you write pages of ranting.

2. *Use Metaphors, not Analogies*

a. Use metaphors as a method to make valid points in support of your argument.

b. Metaphors are more effective than analogies because analogies tend to focus on the differences between two things, whereas a metaphor focuses on the similarity between them.

c. The trick to using metaphors is to use ones that your target audience will understand and relate to. If the reader doesn't understand you point or feel the intended emotion, your efforts are lost.

3. *Bring up the Competition*

a. Discuss your strengths in comparison to your competitor's weaknesses.

b. There is no need to mention any of your competitor's names - it's actually better if you don't. Focus on the products and position yours at an advantage to your competition.

4. *It's About Being Positive*

a. As easy as it is to badmouth the competition, it's best to focus on the positive aspects of your product versus the negative aspects of your competitor's product.

For instance, when comparing the strengths of your product to a competitor's, you could write, "Company X's product is terrible. It's cheaply made and doesn't function like it should."

While this may be true, saying it does 3 things to harm your company and its credibility.

1. Disparaging remarks like this shows that you are unpleasant. Perhaps everyone in the company is like you and difficult to work with.

2. It actually works to discredit your company and add credibility to your competition because it makes you look jealous. And if you're jealous, you must be for a reason - perhaps Company X makes better products?

3. Confuses the reader into wondering why you're bringing up Company X when you should be focusing on your product.

b. The best approach to product or service comparison is to focus on the positive aspects of your product in relation to the competition without mentioning the competition by name, and without being disparaging. Simple enough?

For instance, let's convert the negative statement above into one that will be more advantageous to your company (Company A). "Company A's product is guaranteed to function the way it is intended because of its top of the line parts and talented engineers."

In this statement, you implied that the competitor's product is inferior without pouring scorn on their product. By staying positive, you are exhibiting professional behavior and keeping your reader's focus on your product and your product alone.

Chapter 53
Leveraging the White Paper

The White Paper is an extremely powerful marketing tool when used with effective strategy.

Very Effective leveraging techniques include:

- Third party authorship of your company which implies endorsement and is more effective than self-promotion

- Use as sales training tools

- Addition of new content to a company website, keeping it fresh

- Document that aids in training, recruiting and certification

- Supplying information for newsletters, podcasts and webinars

- Placement of company in strong light for investors and sponsors

- Usage in brochures and tradeshow displays

- Content for public relations

- Source for quotes on other sites or in media, which strengthen the company, further.

Chapter 54
Key Points

> A white paper is used to argue a specific point or explanation to a problem.

> Commercial white papers are close to always used for marketing different types of communication documents that are designed to help promote a company's or groups specific solution or their products.

> The publication of a white paper is to test public opinion in regards to a controversial policy while

helping to enable the government to take a guess at the results.

➤ Remember your goals for the paper before you actually write it.

➤ Overview the Material -Get key points across to the reader

➤ When using metaphors make sure they can and will appeal to all of your readers.

➤ White papers are distributed by our government and help to organize policy on a current topic of concern.

Chapter 55
Review

Now, let's go over the process of writing the White Paper. Answer these questions to review what you've learned.

Questions:

1) What is a white paper?

2) Name 3 differences between a government white paper and a commercial white paper.

3) Looking back to the section "Formatting your white paper," remember to try and control the _____ of your paper.

4) Your white paper should be separated into smaller sections with easy to read _____.

5) What are white papers used for?

6) What are the 4 main types of white papers?

7) Is it a good idea to badmouth your competitors? Explain and defend your position.

8) White papers are distributed by our _____ and help to organize policy on a current topic of concern.

9) Why is it so important to remember your point of topic throughout writing your white paper?

10) Commercial white papers are used as a type of _____tool.

Basic Process

1) How do you choose a topic for your white paper?

2) How do you identify the target reader for your white paper?

3) Who do you conduct interviews with?

4) Why do you Interview customers on their issues and personal beliefs?

5) What documents should you gather and why?

6) Why is it necessary to present your outline, topic and first draft?

7) How do you leverage the white paper?

Chapter 56
Case Studies
(What they are and why you need them)

A case study is one of the most valuable weapons in your armory. Think of it as the story behind your product or brand and how, like a knight in shining armor, it comes to the rescue of a very bother- some problem.

Case studies are used by businesses to highlight their accomplishments. Some people call them "success stories". They are capable of either helping to boost marketing and publicity or completely tear apart a company's credibility, depending on how they are written.

As an example, if you were to write a case study for a company selling scissors, you would want to focus on how the scissors were used by a school's art class for a multiple number of years. You would want to write about how the scissors were used to cut different material, and remained sharp despite being used and "abused" by the students.

In other words, the case study is highlighting the product by telling a story.

Chapter 57
Benefits of Case Studies

1) Adds Credibility to your brand:

Unlike brochures, newsletters and press releases that reflect the company's stance or message, a case study reflects the client's reaction to the product or business. This presents an endorsement and by adding quotes from consumers, acts as testimonials.

2) Connects Problems with Solutions:

Stories of the products and how they solved specific problems or were beneficially used in specific situations, gives perspective clients a good idea of how the products can be applied. If this matches their pain points, the study will pique their interest.

3) Goes Viral to Spread Your Brand:

Ask satisfied clients to review your product and post comments about these reviews on their social media site

4) Works well with Multi-Media Presentations:

Case studies work particularly well in video format as well as print. Seeing a satisfied customer who found a solution by using your product first hand is very powerful. "Seeing is believing."

Reach For the Sky

When writing a case study, try to remember that the sky is the limit when it comes to subject matter. You could be writing about scissors one day, refrigerators the next, computer chips another day, and microprocessors at another time.

A business can have multiple case studies for each of the products from the company. There is no restriction as long as they are not duplicitous.

With case studies, the goal is to take a much larger problem and help break it down into the individual or single unit.

With that being said, the first thing to realize when writing a case study is that it is essential for there to be a problem that the readers can solve. Usually these "problems" already exist.

It's just up to you to do the research behind it and put it together. Just keep in mind that whatever you may choose it has to be true and supported with facts.

A case study is a very detailed piece. It requires extensive research so that statistics can be incorporated into the success stories.

Case studies help highlight many of the common problems and faults in the field (of your choice) and will help solve those problems through the study of its application to specific individuals, companies, and government, or one of whatever it is you choose to study.

Make it short, simple, and sweet. Basically get your point across to the readers without sounding patronizing or trite. Get right to the issue, what was done to try to resolve it, the steps taken by the company, the thought processes of those involved, the proposed solution, and the results.

The thing to remember when discussing products is to present the benefits, not the features. When you mention features, you must take it a step further so that you are answering the "so what".

Tell the reader, not about the feature but what the feature will enable the consumer to do and what pain point it solves.

If you think about it, writing case studies is like writing lab reports -remember science class when you had an introduction, a hypothesis, the materials, methods, data, and results?

Chapter 58
Viewpoints

There are 3 main vantage points by which case studies can be based, when con- structing the case study.

1) The Individual Viewpoint

These usually take into count the individual placement, subjective types of behavior, different types of personality, learning, and interpersonal parts of a specific subject.

2) The Organizational Viewpoint

This focuses on more of an organizational structure or high quality in organizational performance.

3) The Social Viewpoint

This is primarily about different types of urban developments, group habits, and marketplace objectives.

Case Studies are much more flexible with their information purely because there is a broad arrangement of questions that can be asked while narrowing down every possible outcome.

You can look at writing case studies like you're writing a story. You can include characters, dialogue, and a plot. As long as the case study is truthful, based on facts, and grabs the interest of your target audience, you're good to go.

Hook & Reel 'Em In!

Think of it in terms of fishing. Once you've hooked your readers, you want to keep them interested in your story. Reel them in with a proposed solution that readers should agree with - or at least understand how and why that particular solution was reached.

In order to do this it is best to choose a problem that has enough information within it so that readers are able to dissect it after taking time to think about possible solutions and come up with something more concrete.

An example of this would be a case study done on financial information and how it influences decision-making in the corporate world. If you look up the title in any search engine, you'll immediately see just how much information on the web there is on that particular topic.

Additional resources include libraries, financial periodicals and journals, and the best source of information - the company that hired you. More often than not, the company has a plethora of information that you can use. Many times they just don't know it.

Check the customer service, product in- formation, and sales departments. They have tons of information about issues and solutions that many times, the executives don't know.

Now, you have a basic idea or at least an outline of exactly what writing a case study is about, but in order to write a GOOD case study it takes a lot more than just an ex- planation... but we will get to that later.

The Customer Behind the Screen

Nowadays, the research has been greatly facilitated by the Internet. All the information is right in front of you. Clients and perspective consumers can easily be found in forums or chat rooms where they share their problems and complaints.

Matching their problems up with the solutions you can provide makes for a great case study. If you are not sure how to maximize your company's products, reading about what the target market wants, makes writing case studies much easier and more productive.

All types of different businesses use case studies, from huge corporations that market well-known household goods such as Kellogg's cereal and Shell gasoline, to smaller businesses that want to increase their market presence.

Chapter 59
Approaches to Case Studies

Case study topics are not so cut and dry. They can be about how the company developed their existing business leader- ship style, or how your client exhibited environmental awareness and support by organizing a beach or park cleanup day at a local neighborhood.

Other approaches serve:

The Public-

A case study could depict how the company's product helped improve someone's life. The topics surrounding products are limitless.

Academia-

Research is also in need of great case study writers. If you specialized in writing scientific case studies, you could be writing about a current scientific controversy, where your client stands in the argument, how your client tried a proposed solution, and the results of the solution.

Politics-

Case studies can provide the positive publicity so sorely needed and sought by politicians. You can write about how your politician saw a problem in a neighbor- hood, proposed a solution, and how that solution is working for the neighborhood today.

Business Comparisons-

Case studies are also used in business classes as examples of how different companies approached similar problems, the solutions each business came up with, and the results (measured in revenue) that came from each solution. This comparison makes for very interesting reading and helps consumers determine which company suits their needs best.

Chapter 60
First Steps to Writing a Case Study

When writing a Case Study, there are several steps you can take to communicate your message concisely and clearly to your readers without using industry jargon or sounding patronizing and contrite.

Paint a picture of the type of person using the product discussed in the case study. By allowing the readers to envision the type of consumer illustrated, the readers can then put themselves in the main character's shoes (whether that main character is the company or a customer of the company).

The reader must be able to empathize with the voice of the case study, and anticipate the next step - almost like reading an exciting mystery novel.

Most importantly, keep in mind that the goal is to provide information that the reader can easily identify and analyze while coming to a conclusion.

Chapter 61
Steps to Writing Case Studies

There are 3 main steps when writing case studies:

- Research

- Analysis,

- Construction of story from framework of details

Remember that just like in any writing project, you may do research first, then write, then analyze, then research again, analyze again, and finally write again.

Basically, the three steps are mutually exclusive. They can occur at any order, at any time in the process of writing a case study.

Research, Research, and then Research some more

Step 1. The Internet can be a major useful and helpful research tool - when used correctly, of course. Try and figure out what is already out there, highlighting major and important articles that pertain to your case study specifically.

Don't be surprised when you come across an existing problem that may need solving. You also might find that you have to come up with different ideas that may or may not work for your case study.

Example: Issues that affect effective organizing in the work place. The case problem here would to be how to figure out how to solve this to where organization is obtainable in a work place environment while diminishing communication errors, resulting in a more effective workplace.

What to do:

Interview Everyone! Okay, not really "everyone" but people that are knowledgeable about the topic in question.

People who visit and work at the site can also help tremendously with this.

Don't forget your basic 5 "W" questions...

Who?

➢ Who are the major players in this case study?

➢ Who brought up the problem that needed solving?

➢ Who benefitted from the solution?

➢ Who came up with the solution?

What?

➢ What is the problem?

➢ What is the solution?

➢ What are the ramifications - long term and short term of each proposed solution?

Where?

➢ Where did this take place?

➢ Where in the organization do you think adjustments should be made?

When?

➢ When did the problem occur?

➢ When was the solution put into place?

➢ When will we start seeing the benefits or hindrances of the proposed solution?

Why?

➢ Why did the problem occur in the first place?

➢ Why did we choose one solution over another?

➢ Why was this issue considered a priority?

And also, the much neglected, "How?" Many times, case study writers forget that the "how" is just as important as the 5 W's. "How" questions include:

➢ How was the conclusion reached?

➢ How was the decision made - the process, etc.?

➢ How important was this issue to the company?

➢ How fast was the issue resolved?

➢ How would you feel if you were on the other side of the coin?

Step 2: Analysis at its Finest

Sorting through various information that you have now collected through use of the Internet, interviews, books and various other ways of gathering information is a major part of putting together your case writing.

Keep in mind while sorting through all of this you want to keep the information that will be most useful so that the issue will be understandable for readers.

When writing a case study, **although it is important to sift through all of the research you have gathered,** remember that they can involve much more information on the subject being tested than any researcher would like to know - their educational background, personal opinions, likes, and dislikes. It is up to you as the writer, to figure out what information needs to be included in the case study, and what information can be eliminated without compromising the credibility of your client and of the study.

When breaking apart the problem, imagine each piece as part of the original equation. In order to reach the solution, you may find out that you need to spend some more time researching or spending more time discussing it with other groups.

Come up with questions that you are able to ask yourself on how many people and how much information needs to be provided in order to complete your case study. Once you have broken it up into pieces then you can move onto how to put your case study together.

Step 3: Creation- *The Actual Writing Part...*

Once you have managed to come up with what you believe is enough information and organized it to your liking, you can finally start what you thought you were going to be doing all along - writing!

Case studies focus mainly on the context. Specialization comes into place, putting emphasis on various points and being extremely detailed about it.

Start off with **describing your case question** that you want your readers to solve.

Example: In a mystery novel, the crime happens right at the very beginning of the story.

Likewise, with case studies, after you have made it clear what the problem is exactly, you can then move on to quoting different people that you have inter- viewed. Make a question out of different things you have been told.

Try to draw your reader's attention so that their interest isn't lost part way through reading your case. The last thing you want as a case study writer is to not compel your reader to continue reading.

There are a few ways to go about doing just this.

Compel Your Reader to Continue Reading by...

➢ Beginning with organization of the different parts of the case

➢ Including some type of introduction to your case question. This is essential!

➢ Giving some background information on exactly where this is all taking place and add anything that you believe will really help your readers visualize it - an overall description including what makes this place so relevant to your case study.

➢ Putting the case study together, which takes a lot of thought and effort. However, sometimes, instead of handing the reader everything "on a platter," you want to make the reader do a little mental work too.

☐ Let the readers come up with their own conclusions by making comparisons. You can make this possible by adding in information about the people whom you have interviewed - including visitors, what they liked and didn't like.

➢ Readers like to be able to analyze different points of views. Make sure that you include information that is applicable to the situation, specific to the situation, and understandable for a wide array of readers.

➢ The best case studies are ones in which there is something revealed. Keep in mind that it's all about the results. Before you are able to come up with a result, it is vital to set it up so that the reader is entranced by your words - by the story you are telling - and to keep that level of intrigue until the very end when you reveal the conclusion.

➢ In order to have a great case study, your content should not only fascinate your readers but also challenge them, at least just a bit. Along with that there should be a sequence of different thoughts and actions that eventually will lead to a conclusion.

Chapter 62
6 Step Formula to Success

There is a simple formula to having your case study appeal to readers...

1) Determine what your case will be about then make sure that all of your information is organized is such a way that readers can easily identify with what the issue at hand is while also coming to a conclusion about it.

2) Secondly, choose a "case site".

  - Think of a location, an organization, company, or someone who is dealing with that problem.

  - Then go ahead and set up interviews with these people.

Everyone that you interview should be involved with the same company or organization (your case "site").

They can be workers, volunteers, or customers, with an interest in solving the problem you have chosen.

3) Begin your interviewing process! Talk to individuals at your case site about the problem you chose.

4) Analyze the information that you have put together through various research

5) Write the case study! Making sure it has the following information:

- Introduction to the problem

- Background on the case

- The next several sections should be specifically about the problem as it pertains to the case

- Lastly, make sure that whatever your conclusion might be that it is satisfying for a general audience and leaving it open for the reader to come up with a possible different conclusion

6) Remember that the objective here is to feature your organization's overall capabilities while solving a general business problem.

Chapter 63
Case Study: The good vs. the bad

As mentioned before, case studies can basically determine life or death for a company's credibility.

It has been noted by some that most case studies analyze much more detailed information than just plain research alone. They are able to deal with much more de- tailed information using more creativity and context.

On the other hand, some like to argue that case studies are too difficult to generalize purely because all the information given is subjective and one sided, focusing mainly on particular types of content.

What is a Problem without a Solution?

Be consistent with organizing your information. Whatever you decide to write about, make sure to stick with it. Make sure to organize your information in such a way to where it is easy enough for your readers to identify what is going on. By doing this, not only does it make your case study easier for the reader to grasp but it also makes it easier for you to write.

Now that you have mastered the task of Case Story writing, you should be able to go out there and create masterpieces with ease. Just remember to practice, practice, and practice. Write, write, and write.

Before deciding to throw yourself out there though, take a look at some main points and questions, then we will be able to move on to the next task at hand.

Chapter 64
Tips and Points to Ponder

> Writing not only a case study but also a ***good*** one there are several tips to making this possible.

- Problem & Solution

- Research, research, RESEARCH!

- Incorporating enough information to where the readers can easily identify what is going on.

- Interviewing the people that know the place the best will be most beneficial to your case story

- Use lots of detail when putting your setting together for your case story

> Organize your case into different sections

> Give background information on where and what this place is about

> Don't give your readers all of the answers; make them do a little work too.

> Don't forget to include a hook for your readers right away so that you're able to keep their attention throughout the Case Study

> Your case NEEDS a conclusion, but rather than just giving it to readers ask more questions that will lead them to their own conclusion

> Make sure that your Case Study can appeal to most if not all audiences.

Chapter 65
Review of What You Have Learned

Fill in the answers to reinforce the information you have absorbed.

Questions:

1) What is a Case Study?

2) List the three most common bases that are covered when writing a case study.

3) When writing a case study the goal is to provide enough _____ that the reader can easily identify and analyze while coming to a conclusion.

4) Name one good and one bad thing about writing a case study.

5) Be _____ when organizing your information for your readers.

a. Short

b. Consistent

c. Brief

6) What is the 4 step Formula to success?

7) The best case studies are ones in which something is _____

8) What are the three main steps to writing a case study?

9) What is one key concept to keep in mind when writing a case study?

10) How is giving background information on your case study helpful to the reader?

PODCASTS
THE NEXT BIG WAVE!

Chapter 66
The New World

We live in exciting times where it seems that there is a new development in technology or some new method popping up almost daily...and to be successful, you must be adopting them.

Clients want to do business with companies who are on the cutting edge. That now means that a business must be able to interact with perspective leads and customers by more than just reading web content.

Websites must include videos or an audio tool for more active communications. If you are not involved with any interactive tool, the perception is that you are "old school" which does not bode well for your business.

The solution to this problem is developing pod-casts. Enabling clients to download your sound file, you can now spread your message through an iPod, smart phone or mp3 player while they exercise, walk or commute to work.

Podcasts have been around for several years now (formerly called audioblogging) and yet people still tend to get confused about what a podcast exactly is.

Chapter 67
What is a Podcast?

Podcasts, formerly called webcasts, can be either audio or video. They are series of digital media files. They are released by the creator of the programs and files on a regular basis and downloaded by smart devices for listening or watching. Often, these programs are distributed through web syndication.

Unlike streamed webcasting, the files lie on the distributor's server. The audience utilizes a specific application software system, referred to as a podcatcher, which allows access to the web feed and new file, download. In a sense, this is more like newspapers or magazines than radio, which is a live stream.

Audio file formats generally used are:

- **MP3-** a system of compression for audio signals. The redundant or irrelevant segments of sound signals are deleted from the third layer to transmit a clear recording, void of superfluous noise. Special filters achieve resolution of the sound. This format is played on MP3 players- portable electronic devises that enable storage and play backs of music or video files.

- **Ogg Vorbis-** an audio compression format system. Ogg stands for the Ogg Project, an Open Source multimedia initiative. Vorbis is the actual compression format. What makes this system unique is that it is open and free for usage with no patent encumbrances. The system is located on the public domain and is available for both personal and commercial use.

According to the Journalism & Communication Research group at the University of Texas at Austin, a podcast which is a "digital or video file is comprised of 4 parts:

1. episodic

2. downloadable

3. Program-driven (with host and/or theme)

4. Convenient (via automated feed interfaced with computer software)"

A simple way to describe this is that a podcast is an audio or video program or file that has been pre-recorded and posted online. It's accessible by download to listen or view through mobile devices or the computer.

So...anything audio that's online is a podcast, right?

Ever since the technology has come about to make it possible, people have been producing audio and video files and posting it online.

This is NOT podcasting, my friend.

Why?

One very important element is missing. In order to make posted audio and video files an actual podcast, the proper technology needs to be involved to allow automated content downloading and syndication.

What this means is that a podcaster – one who records and distributes podcasts can solicit subscriptions from his or her listeners. These subscriptions can be paid, or they can be free, in exchange for contact information such as the name and email of the subscriber.

The benefit of subscribing to a podcast series is to have each new episode automatically delivered to you via electronic media. How often these are delivered de- pends on the podcast series. Sometimes delivery is weekly, other times monthly, daily, or even sporadically.

The idea is to subscribe so you can find out what happens next in the series.

As a podcaster, the reason behind having subscribers to your podcast is to gain a following and build your database. The more interesting you are, the more sub- scribers you will get. This enables you to sell to a larger market through the podcast and also have the contact information to add to your website list as well.

Podcasts use software such as iTunes along with others to automatically down- load to a computer that then can be placed otherwise known as "synched" onto a portable media device such as an iPod. This auto downloading has caused podcast consumption to skyrocket.

As a result, almost all portable media players made today can be synchronized with podcasts.

Chapter 68
RSS, XML

Podcasting uses a precise process called Really Simple Syndication, abbreviated as RSS. (This technology is also utilized by blogs).

What are RSS & XML?

RSS is a technology gives the subscriber a way to receive updated information automatically and in a standard format (XML).

Good illustrations of RSS are represented by popular news publications such as The Wall Street Journal, which provides news stories to many RSS directories.

These directories distribute the stories throughout the Internet. If you want to read the articles, they are accessible via an RSS-enabled Web browser or similar programs that are specially designed to retrieve RSS feeds.

XML stands for Extensible Markup Language. According to Wikipedia, XML is "a set of rules for encoding documents in machine-readable form." Similar to HTML (Hyper Text Markup Language – pretty much how everything online is visible to you as words and not gobbledy- gook), XML is designed to carry data – not display it.

XML doesn't actually DO anything. It was simply developed and designed to create structure, and function as a way to store and transport information.

Chapter 69
Benefits

Podcasts enables you to take your message to the next level.

After you have mastered article publication, blogging, ezines and social media, the next step to reach a new market that you may not have tapped into yet for potential leads or lead con-version, is the medium of podcasts. This tool complements your other marketing strategies.

A report issued by Edison Research claims that almost half of Americans over age 12 (70 million) have listened to or watched a minimum of one podcast over the last year.

Business Benefits of Podcasts include:

- **Reaching New Audiences in your target market**

  Millions of people are active on social media sites with 177 million tweets daily and more than 75% of the world's population posting entries on Face- book.

  But the key word here is "active". Just as a certain segment enjoys listening to audio books rather than actively reading them, or have their content come to them instead of actively asking questions in forums and chat rooms, these same people in the population want to "listen in" for their information.

  The thing is, while audiences click a selection to hear a podcast, the selection number is limited as opposed to standard media chan- nels. The field is still wide open to developing your own podcasts and sending your mes- sage out into the airwaves.

- **Strengthening Brand Recognition**

  The more places that people see your logo, message, voice, name or other representa- tions of your business that can be recognized and linked to you, the stronger your brand becomes.

Simply put, brand recognition is the level at which the public can identify a company by its features or intellectual property. When the general public can recall a brand simply by hearing or seeing associated characters like logos, taglines, slogans, colors, voices and programs, then the brand increases revenue and grows exponentially.

By having podcast programs on a regular basis, your message is spread and you stay in the minds of your current contacts while attracting a new audience and new leads.

- **Increasing Online Traffic**

  Podcasts link to your website, increasing search engine ranking while simultaneously creating fresh material on your site.

  With discussed topics laden with your targeted keywords, you further improve the association of these keywords with you and enhance your search engine optimization (SEO).

Chapter 70
How To Set Up Your Podcast

There is no limit to the types of shows that you can create for a podcast. If a topic interests you and helps spread your message, chances are someone else is interested too- helping to gather new leads, new fans, and new clients.

So, how do you get started podcasting?

For practical purposes, you need the right equipment for:

- Recording capabilities and usage of these sound files

- Ability to answer interactive calls, filtering out spam or unwanted callers

- Mute callers until individual engagement is allowed

- Offer with RSS feed directories (like iTunes) can syndicate and distribute the podcast to subscribers

- Setup of live stream if live broadcast is desired A helpful resource that I would like to recommend is Talkshoe.com

This free website enables you to simultaneously broadcast live and record the program for distribution. Alteration of the program is possible by downloading the sound file, editing the areas in question and reuploading the show. Sound files are immediately archived, allowing clients to either stream the program through their computer or download it onto their mobile devices.

Chapter 71
Creating a Podcast

Start off by answering these questions and making a list.

1. Goal-

What is the objective of the podcast?

2. Frequency-

How often will the podcast be? Make sure that you are consistent here. If a fan wants to hear the program through a live streaming mode, don't disappoint this fan and essentially turn away interested individuals, unlikely to return.

3. Theme-

What the theme of your podcast? Does it reflect your brand? Does it tie into goods and services that you are promoting? Will you be able to use the information as fresh content on your website?

4. Format-

What format you might distribute your pod-cast in? This just depends on what theme you choose and the technology that you are com-fortable with using.

5. Hardware-

If you don't already have the necessary gear to begin a podcast, you either need to invest in the basic gear - a computer with Internet access, a microphone, and headphones - or invest in a computer that already contains these items. Keep in mind that these are the basic tools. If you want to include video, you'll need the proper equipment for that as well.

Chapter 72
The 4 Ps of a Good Podcast

Before you start talking, you should have an outline of sorts – to prevent babbling, and all other annoying speaking quirks you may have.

So, let's look at the structure of a good podcast.

The 4 P's:

1. Planning

2. Producing

3. Publishing

4. Promoting

1. Plan out your Podcast

It's easy to get excited and carried away with the idea of getting your voice out there on the web but planning ahead of time will help you stay focused on what needs to be accomplished.

In the end you will be able to produce a much better podcast that will also attract and keep more listeners.

Here are a few things you need to think about for your podcast:

• What's the topic for your podcast?

• What's the format of your podcast?

• How long will each of your episodes be?

• How often do you plan on releasing new shows?

Choose a topic for your podcast that you're actually interested in and that you enjoy talking about, something that excites you and keeps your interest.

Before you record each of your episodes, it would be most beneficial to write up an outline. You don't have to have anything elaborate. A simple list of the things that you'll include in your show is fine.

An outline also helps you stay on track and not lose your place in the middle of recording.

Having an outline will actually make it easier to help create your show notes later, show notes are an outline of what is in the show to help listeners see what they can expect to hear.

Even if your podcast is as simple as just you talking without any clips or music, it is still a good idea to give a little thought to what it is exactly that you plan on saying. You want to make sure to have a quality show that will bring even more listeners back.

Create an outline in whatever way works for you best. Just remember that it needs to be easy for you to read as you are recording.

2. Producing your Podcast

Producing your podcast just consists of actually doing it – be it talking, singing, yodeling, reading, or making animal noises. It's the meat of your podcast.

Remember to keep your mind on your audience. If they are professionals, they probably want to hear a professional. Mind your language and your stutters.

Consider having interviews. This is a great way to demonstrate your authority while having someone else do the talking, helping to relieve the pressure of being the sole content creator.

Engage your listeners. Have them call in and ask questions, which creates con- tent, not only for the specific show, but also as a basis for a future show. This also lures listeners into tuning into a new show to hear a continuation of a program that was of interest to them.

3. Publishing your Podcast

Once you've created your first podcast, you have to be able to prepare it for publishing and posting it onto the Internet.

To publish your podcast to the Internet:

1. Register a Web Address (this is also called a domain name)

2. Find/Buy Web Hosting (this is to help store your blog and or site and your audio files onto the internet)

3. Start a Blog (this is your personal web site for posting your show notes, links, and anything else)

4. Create an RSS Feed (this is the feed that your listeners will subscribe to so they can automatically download new episodes of your podcast straight to there mp3's)

4. Promoting your Podcast

➢ The first step in promoting your podcast has to do with the description of the podcast itself. Your podcast description should be clear and give an accurate representation of the contents of your podcast.

➢ The next step in promoting your podcast is to get it out there; there are tons of sites that list podcasts. There are podcast directories, forums that discuss podcasts and then there are the search engines also.

➢ The last step is being able to manage the growth. If you by chance make it to this step you should know that this is where you will have an ever increasing number of listeners and may even attain cult status for your podcast.

Chapter 73
Guide for Domain Selection
http://www.keywordPodcast.com

Suffixes

This is the ending of a URL designating location. There are many suffixes to choose from:

- com

- org

- usa

- net

- me

Most people automatically type in .com and so you should try to have a domain name with this suffix.

If someone else has the name that you would like but the .com is taken, it is really not a good idea to choose the same name with a different suffix. You will confuse your fans that will automatically go into .com by default and you will be promoting someone else's business.

As a rule, when you register the name that you would like, it is a good idea to buy the same name with several different suffixes so that no one else can purchase your name and "ride on your coattails".

Keywords

Choose a name that has your keywords in them. It will be easier for everyone to associate you with it, helping further your branding and will help increase search engine rankings for you on that keyword. When people search under a particular topic, your domain name is working for you in promotion because it pops up on the first page of the search.

Make the name meaningful to your target market. Figure out what they are searching for and place this in your name. This increases the chances of being found when they are looking.

Length

Don't make the address too long. The shorter it is, the easier it is to remember. Also the longer the name is, the higher the chances are for type mistakes or spelling mistakes when entering the name while searching for you.

Consistency

Make the name of the website and the name of the podcast the same. This further strengthens the brand and does not lead to confusion.

Availability

"Great minds think alike". It is very possible that someone else has already chosen the name that you have selected. You can check web address availability on 000domains.

There are many places to register the domain name. A very popular site is http://www.GoDaddy.com. While they may not be the least expensive, they have a very good technical support system and offer several other services and templates in addition to domain registration

Chapter 74
Storage

The minimum size of the storage needed is 1000 megabytes (MB) or one gigabyte (GB). This will supply enough room for the audio files, website, blog posts and images.

Keep in mind that you will need stor- age for the shows available online and the ones that are archived.

Storage demands will vary depending on:

- Quality-The greater the quality, the more space it takes on files

- Frequency of show production

- Length of each show

- How many shows are available to listeners at any given time.

Because raw files (the initial recording) take up too much space, the sound files are converted to MP3 format (compressing or encoding files)

File compression

Files are squashed or converted to ten percent of the original size, which enables easier uploading onto the Internet. How- ever, you are trading ease of transfer and speed with quality. The more compression there is, the more the audio quality is sacrificed.

Bit Rate

This is a measure of data is number of bits that gets processed over a given period of time (each second). In general, the higher the bitrate used, the higher the quality of sound when played back.

The bitrate of CDs is more than ten times that of the best MP3 recording (but perhaps not as convenient).

Chapter 75
Podcast Promotion

Developing and publishing your podcasts are relatively easy in comparison to getting listeners for the program.

In order to amass an audience, there needs to be a strategy that you formulate to let everyone know you're present, live and available.

Steps for Podcast Success

1) Establish an Email List

Send reminders to your listeners. There are so many attention-getters throughout each day that even ardent fans need to be reminded of upcoming program broadcasts.

2) Add Tags (with Keywords) to the Text Description

Search engines (like Technorati) need words to find the sound files. Adding tags makes the search more significant and should encompass the specific episode discussed.

E.g. Let's say that you have a podcast about healthcare and in one show you focus on patient advocacy. The links would appear as follows:

<a href="http://technorati.com/tag/ health-care" rel="tag">healthcare</a>

<a href="http://technorati.com/tag/ patient+advocacy" rel="tag">patient advocacy</a>

rel="tag" lets the search engines know that this link is a tag. Inserting a plus sign (+) denotes two words with a space in be- tween for the tag.

3) Be consistent with your website SEO

Link the podcast to your online site. Announce the podcast on the website and give a summary or highlight of the upcoming show. This can be done with a quick video trailer as well. The purpose of this is to lure the audience to the next episode. It will also help the spiderbots find you on the search engines.

4) Send Press Releases-

A powerful, yet underutilized marketing tool, press releases lets everyone know about your podcast and garner new ears to your program. Contests and celebrity interviews make great press releases as well as cover- age of breaking news and hot current topics.

5) Index Your Podcast-

When an online service gets a subscriber to a podcast, it indexes the program, making it easier to find...even when you are the subscriber!

Subscribe to the following sites:

☐ Bloglines

☐ Yahoo

☐ AOL

☐ MSN Google Reader

☐ Odeo

6) List Yourself in Directories-

There is a vast array of directories available. By registering your feed to every RSS directory available to you, the chances of being found and gaining new listeners soars.

There are many lists available but the one that was compiled by Robin Good is an outstanding list of 55 places to submit your feed.

Do a Google search for all the directories that you can find. The two most popular are:

http://www.ipodlounge.com and http:// www. ipodcasting.meetup.com

Chapter 76
Sponsorship

CONTACT ALL THE CO.S THAT
STAND TO PROFIT

Let's face it. You are paying for the domain each month, added up the expense for all the hardware that you've invested in, paid the host server each month and dollars are flying out the window...lots of them!

Getting sponsors for the podcast or radio show is a great solution to getting a subsidy for your efforts and. ...Maybe even a profit!

How to Get Sponsors

Study your podcasts and think of whom the ideal advertisers would be. Which companies would profit most from sharing the tar- get market that makes up your audience?

There is a hugh pool of potential sponsors in podcasts that focus on a particular topic or field. Think of who stands to gain and whose branding being associated with you will strengthen.

A good illustration of this is as follows:

You have a podcast each week on car mechanics and fixing what goes wrong with cars. Potential sponsors might be car insurance agencies, car warranty companies, fuel additives, etc. See the connection?

Sponsorship Offers

Advertisers need to know exactly what you are offering. Putting a package together allows them to see exactly what they are getting and allows them to measure the value of it. (Which you should be pointing out to them in your offer)

Also stress the value of name-dropping in archived episodes, which are downloaded numerous times over the initial show for additional coverage of the sponsor.

Package Offerings:

- Number of live mentions that the podcast gives

- Banner ads on website or blog

- Ads in show's email campaigns

- Reviews of sponsor's goods and services

- Segments of shows that mention the sponsor as "brought to you by"

- Run contests and prizes with gifts by the sponsors- and mentions

Don't stop looking for sponsors just because you have some. Mention that there are sponsorship opportunities available both on your blog posts, email campaigns for the podcast show and on the shows themselves.

Place the information prominently in a sidebar.

Chapter 77
Key Information

4 Basic Steps

1) Register a domain name (your URL or web address) E.g. www.Yourshow.com

2) Get Web Hosting where the sound files and blogs will be stored

3) Create a blog- to post episodes and links to shows

4) Establish an RSS feed for the audience to subscribe and get automatic downloads.

Remember the 4 P's:

- Planning

- Producing

- Publishing

- Promoting

Creating a podcast is a five-step process

1. Create your audio file

2. Upload your audio file

3. Create your show notes on your website

4. Create and publish your RSS feed

5. Tell everyone you know where to find your RSS feed

Chapter 78
Review

See how much you've learned by reviewing the questions

Questions:

1. What is a Podcast?

2. What does RSS stand for and what is its purpose?

3. What does XML stand for and what is its purpose?

4. List the 4 P's with a brief description of each?

5. Why should you choose a topic in which you're interested in when it comes to making a podcast?

6. Is creating an outline a good idea even if you only plan on talking during the podcast? Why?

7. True or False, It doesn't matter what type of computer you have to create a podcast because there is no specific equipment needed.

8. Before you record each of your episodes, it would be most beneficial to write up a

   _____.

9. Choose a topic for your podcast that you're _____ interested in.

10. Once you've created your first podcast, you have to be able to prepare it for _____.

Chapter 79
Press Releases

What exactly is a press release?

Simply put, a press release is a communication either in writing or a recorded message to members of the media, letting them know a newsworthy item.

Generally, they are sent to assignment editors at radio and television stations, newspapers and magazines and written by copywriters.

Media is driven by buzz and news so that getting a compelling or enticing piece of information helps them perform their job and is appreciated. Taking the nuggets of information, the editors can flesh out interesting stories and expand upon them (good for them and great for you!)

The trick is getting your information compelling and enticing. In other words, make your communication "newsworthy".

Because of the Internet, there are hundreds of distribution sites; some of these services are free, others are quite afford- able for the smaller businesses or healthcare practices.

Newsworthy information includes announcements of:

- Events

- Products

- New Discoveries

- Change of Management

- Economic changes

- Awards

- Accomplishments

Press Statement

Information fed to reporters, this is issued to media for distribution to the public.

Alternate names for press releases:

- News release

- Press statement

- Video release

- Media release

A press release is a short yet very compelling news story written by a public relations person and then sent to targeted members of the media.

Because publicity is not only a cost- effective marketing strategy but also a great way to build credibility, press releases are a fantastic way for a company to get a foot up over the competition and build credibility through positive publicity.

Press releases differ from advertising because advertising controls the message. That is, when you see an ad for a product, you know that it is a subjective point of view, beneficial to the company making the product.

A press release is something that is published by the media - something that most of us still view as having an objective opinion.

When the media publishes your story, it exposes your company to the masses, thus potentially increasing your marketing reach, sales revenue, and ultimately, the bottom line. If you write this story, you become the company's superstar.

Sound like something you want to do? Read on. It's probably one of the easiest ways to combine journalistic writing with marketing skills. If this is something that makes your skin tingle with excitement and get your writing hand to itch with anticipation, Press Release writing might just be what you're looking for.

Chapter 80
Advantages of Press Releases

Whether introducing a new product or service, launching a company or book, press releases are among the most economical ways to get the word out without spending boat loads of cash on advertising and marketing. Done correctly, this marketing tool can bring in millions in revenue.

9 Benefits

Additional benefits that press releases offer are as follows.

1. Branding

A press release that is picked up and broadcast virally across the internet and multiple media channels, significantly strengthens your brand, company, goods and services, making them well-known.

2. Exposure

Your business, products and services gain more visibility.

3. SEO

As the press release is viewed across the internet on various sites and multi- ple channels, links are created between them and your website, increasing your ranking which further makes you more visible.

4. Targets designated audience

Rather than spending money on generic advertising, press releases hone in on your target market. Press release distribution sites provide for allocation to certain audiences based on demo- graphics and geographical location.

5. Increases leads

When the press releases are syndicated, a larger audience views the news that you want to broadcast out, whether it be a new product, an award that you or your company has received, or the launch of a new business or service.

6. Improves conversion of leads

The fact of the matter is that as we have all heard now, "People do business with those that they know, trust and like." By having increased visibility, and having the first page or first spot in searches online, the perception is that you are more trustworthy and more highly valued.

7. Improves ROI (return on investment)

Press releases give "more bang for your buck". There are free distribution sites if there is no money in your budget for advertising or sites (like PR web) that have very reasonable plans for pack- age deals on multiple press releases over a given period of time.

In contrast to the amount of money that would need to be spent in advertising for the same exposure, press releases are very reasonable so that the net amount the business generates or the bottom line is significantly higher.

8. Enhances social media connections

When your name or the name of your company goes viral and you are well represented across the media channels, people want to connect with you or become your friend.

Everyone loves a winner and wants to be associated with one. You are also perceived, as an authority in your field and people will want to connect with you to get your advice or hear your solutions to the problems that they are struggling with.

9. Increased response

When a professional copywriter creates the press release, the response is greater and media are more inclined to "pick it up" for production of news stories or articles in newspapers or magazines.

Chapter 81
How to Write a Press Release

There are templates or standard formats for writing a press release.

They usually consist of the following elements:

FOR IMMEDIATE RELEASE

All press releases begin with the above words.

Headline

The headline is the single most important line of text in the entire press release. It is what catches the reader's eye first and is also what tells people exactly what the press release is about

It can be an extremely effective tool to help grab attention of journalists, so making sure to write your press release from a journalist's perspective is very important to remember. So start to think exactly what headlines catch your eyes in the newspaper the most.

It's difficult at times to not fall into the cheesy salesman headline trap - especially when you want a title that is compelling and attention grabbing.

For instance, when writing a press re- lease about a new fish oil supplement that doesn't leave a fishy aftertaste in your mouth and is made with all-natural ingredients, some of us might be tempted to write something more sensational like, "Wow! New Fish Oil Pill Tastes Great - Just Like Candy!"

While this does attract the attention of some, its sensationalistic view makes it unbelievable, and will probably not make it to press. Remember that the journalist does not care if your client makes money. The journalist cares if he or she can get a good story out of what you have written so that the editor stays happy.

So if you keep it simple, concise, and truthful, it might intrigue a journalist enough to actually print the piece, thus adding to the publicity of your client.

You could write, "All Natural Fish Oil Leaves No Fishy Aftertaste". It's short, simple, and truthful. And it still is interesting enough to attract your existing as well as potential au- dience. Most importantly, a journalist will find this compelling enough to print.

As for length of headline, try to keep it under 8 words. Anything more will be too long.

The Subhead

Don't discount the value of a well-written subhead. These are very useful tools that are often overlooked. This section basically works to explain the title and set the mood of the rest of the document.

It explains the headline a bit more in detail, amplifies your message, and works to focus the reader to what you want them to read.

Keep this under 300 characters.

An alternative to a subhead is a summary. This should also be concise - one to three descriptive sentences about the subject of the press release.

City, State, Date

This is another standard press release for- mat component. It's important to inform the reader where this is happening and when.

The Lead

The lead paragraph is the first paragraph of your press release. It contains, in a nutshell, what the release is all about. In Journalism 101, the lead contains the following essential information: Who, What, When, Where, and How.

Again, it's important to just keep to the facts. Since a press release is short (nothing more than 500 words), there is no room for fluff or hype. Just say what needs to be said, and say it quick, or your busy journalist will lose interest and your client gets nothing.

Body

The body of the press release contains several components.

Details

The details obviously come after the lead paragraph (also known as the introductory paragraph). It helps give further explanation, statistics, background, or other details relevant to the news this way and also helps back up whatever claims you made in your lead.

Typically the body should be at least 3000 characters or around 500 words (including the lead). Keep the paragraphs short and to the point.

Boilerplate/About the Company

The boilerplate is usually a very short section that provides background information about the company or organization. This is used on every press release submitted.

Media Contacts

This section is what holds all of the con- tact information such as name, phone number, email address, mailing address, etc.... for the media relation's person.

Chapter 82
PRESS RELEASE TEMPLATE

This is a typical press release.

(The company logo can be seen on top of the page.)

FOR IMMEDIATE RELEASE

The Title of Your Press Release Will Go Here in Bold Type

When you distribute a news release, it is helpful to also have a descriptive subhead or a short summary of 1-4 descriptive sentences.

City, State – Date – Type the first paragraph (lead) of the body of your press release here. This paragraph should very briefly answer the questions of whom? What? When?, Why?, and Where?

The second paragraph of the body of your press release should elaborate on your news, and give further details.

Continue with short paragraphs to dis- cuss different aspects of your company or site's news. Limit the length of each paragraph to 2-4 lines each.

You can also include a statement from a company representative or someone that is relevant to the story being told.

You can include a brief summary after the details of your press release.

About Your Company

You should include a boilerplate (it should be the same on every press release you send) with a basic description of who you are and what you do. Give relevant statistics, or any information that makes you seem newsworthy in a general sense (being a major international organization, a published author, etc.). For more information about Your Company/Site or (specific news, product, etc. in the release), please contact Your Name at Your Phone Number.

Contact Info:

Contact Name Company Name Mailing Address City / State / Zip (or City / Country) Phone: Your Phone Number

Email: Your Email Address Web: Your Website URL ### (Indicates end of press release)

Chapter 83
Press Release Distributors

For the budget - restricted businesses, there are several free distribution sites, which carry with it some small restrictions or caveats.

For the complete novice see **PRUrgent. com.** It offers instruction on writing press releases complete with downloadable samples to try your hand with in addition to distributing your finished release.

Additional Free Sites to check out:

NewswireToday.com: (it's premium service permits additional features such as logo insertion, photograph of products and a few more perks)

PR.com: complete company profile per- mitted along with press release distribution.

PRBuzz.com: distributes free to search engines, blogs and various news sites.

PRLog.org: also distributes free to Google News and various other search engines.

24-7 PressRelease.com: free release distribution with stipulation of ad support

1888PressRelease.com: their premium services provides permanent archiving and optimal placement

EcommWire.com: deals with ecommerce and must include links, image and 3 key- words of theirs

Express-Press-Release.com: located in 12 states

ClickPress.com: distributes to Google News and Topix.net. Their paid gold level supplies additional sites (e.g.LexisNexis)

Free-Press-Release-Center.info: Gives a web page with one keyword link to your site along with release distribution. Their pro upgrade supplies three links and permanent archiving with additional perks.

i-Newswire.com: distributes to search engines and various sites. The premium membership provides ability to add graphics

PR9.net: add supported distribution **PR-inside. com:** European based site

PRCompass.com: distribution with a twist. It can be upgraded with popular votes.

Press-Base.com: release submission for their front page and the category selection is yours to make

PressAbout.com: press release is distributed in blog format

PressMethod.com: services dependent on contribution size

PRLeap.com: distributes to search engines, RSS feeds and newswires. Premium cate- gory gives better placement

TheOpenPress.com: distributes plain- for- matted releases. HTML-coded releases are in their paid service.

Paid press releases offer additional services like better placement, graphics and no ads. They usually carry packages offering a certain amount of releases distributed over a period of time. The one most popularly used is PRWeb.com

Chapter 84
Helpful tips

A press release should be written in the third person. Instead of using we, us and ours, use they, them and theirs.

It can be VERY useful to look at other people's press releases. Take the time to look at the most viewed press releases, as they usually provide a lot of insight into how to write a well organized and well- written press release.

Remember that the main goal of a press release is to spark the interest of a journalist or publication. Keep the hype to a minimum. Focus on facts.

Becoming a Successful Press Release Writer

So here it is...writing an effective press release really involves developing a story idea that's not only unique but also timely and newsworthy

Basically a press release won't spark any interest of journalists unless it has to do with something truly original or is closely tied to current events.

Several different factors can make a story newsworthy.

➢ Timeliness is the MOST important. Without this, the story wouldn't be called "news."

➢ Next is the importance of the people or organization that are featured in the story.

➢ Thirdly, the story actually appeals to the intended audience and applies to human-interest in general. (These are stories that are usually very emotional in content).

➢ Lastly, find specific media personal and journalists that would be most interested in your story. Usually journalist's work covering a certain type of news such as sports, food, or politics. So figure out what journalists would be willing to cover your story - otherwise you are most likely going to be ignored.

But I Don't Know Any Journalists!

No need to fret. There are numerous ways to helping to find the right journalist for your story. The method you choose will depend on how many people you want to actually go about contacting.

If your story isn't time sensitive and consists of mostly local interest, you could actually read the local papers while looking for reporters who write about similar topics!

If your story is of national or international interest, send the press release to as many media outlets and journalists as possible. I know that's common sense, but it has to be mentioned.

Believe it or not but there are paid press release services that actually broadcast different story ideas to hundreds if not thousands of journalists all at once. You can write the release and submit it (many are online). They take care of the distribution for you.

Keep in mind that journalists are human beings just like the rest of us and are more likely to look over a press release from a "friend" than from a complete stranger. That's why it is so important to create professional relationships with members of the media!

Chapter 85
Types

6 Different Types of Press Releases

1. General News

A general press release is by far the most common type of press release. This is what first comes to mind when someone hears the words, "press release". Typically this type of press release includes news that must be announced to the media immediately. The objective of this type of press release is to generate interest, cov- erage and exposure for the company that decided to distribute the press release to begin with.

2. Launch

A launch press release is actually pretty similar to that of a general news release in terms of format, but its intent is much, much, much more specific.

A launch press release is a lot more urgent while its main purpose is to create a buzz regarding a specific revelation. This includes announcing a new company, organization, website or any sort of initiative.

3. Product

A product press release often at times comes in a format that is a lot different from a general news release. This is only because a product press release usually includes product specifications.

A product press release can be used together with a launch release if the focus is launching a product. A product press release is the type of press release that would create and distribute if you intend to launch a new product.

4. Executives or Staff Announcement

An executive or staff announcement news release is what you would typically send out if there were staff changes in a company.

This type of press release is different from a general news release in the sense that it can actually contain biographical information to support the other information

5. Expert Positioning

An expert positioning press release is a lot less urgent compared to a regular general news release. Specifically this type of press release can actually focus on a company report and include statistics and or results. Also it may contain news from other organizations.

6. Event

An event press release has an even more different format than a general news release basically because it needs to be shown to members of the media the questions of who, what, when, where and why. Usually an event press release looks a lot like a list or outline instead of paragraphs.

After learning a little more about Press Releases take some time to look over some key points.

Chapter 86
Key Points

➤ A press release is a short yet very compelling news story written by a public relations person and then sent to targeted members of the media.

Remember the several different factors can make a story newsworthy!

- ➢ Timeliness is the MOST important

- ➢ The importance of the people or organization that are featured in the story

- ➢ The story needs to ACTUALLY appeal to the intended audience

- ➢ Make sure to find specific media and journalists that would be most interested in your story.

- ➢ A dateline is what contains the release date of the press release and mostly contains the originating city of the press release.

- ➢ The headline is the single most important line of text in the entire press release, it's what catches people's eye first and is also what tells people exactly what the press release is about.

- ➢ Your headline should be very descriptive but not TOO long

- ➢ An effective press release really involves developing a story idea that's not only unique but also timely and newsworthy

Chapter 87
Review

Answer these questions to review what you've learned.

Questions:

1) What is a press release?

2) What is the single most common type of press release and why?

3) What does an effective press release include?

4) Name 4 different ideas from Chapter 6 that can help your story become news worthy.

5) Typically a press release should be written in _____ person.

6) What is a media contact and why is it so important?

7) What does the "about" section include?

8) Why is the headline so important?

9) What are the 6 different types of press releases?

10) A product press release can be used together with a launch release if the focus is _____ a product.

TECHNICAL WRITING
MADE EASY

Chapter 88
Avoid Costly Mistakes in Technical Writing

We're going to talk about Technical Writing here. You'll discover what it is, how to break into the niche, tips on how to write a great technical document, and the benefits of branching off into this segment of copywriting.

What Is Technical Writing?

The discipline of writing technical documents in a way that is understandable to laymen has been around for a long time. It appeared in the First World War when the military, along with other industries like manufacturing, aerospace, and electronics, had a need for it.

Technical Writing has come a long way since its origins, and has branched off into different niches within the discipline.

Today, technical writers produce documents for numerous industries, including, but not limited to: telecommunication, business, computer hardware, computer software, aerospace, finance, biotechnology, electronics, robotics, and engineering.

Technical writers take a complex idea such as industry-related technology and the jargon typically associated with it, transforming it into something that non- technical people can understand. The key is to do so without changing the main idea presented by the technical document.

An example of a technical document is instructions on how a consumer can operate his or her smart phone. Personally,

I think we need more capable technical writers. I don't know who wrote the instructions to my SmartPhone, but I'm still trying to figure it out!

Requirements for technical writing

In order to be a technical writer, one should:

- Be able to communicate well with a myriad of people types

- Be very detail-oriented

- Like to write

- Have a passion for or aptitude in technology

Knowledge required in certain fields for which technical writing is performed on specific products, comes from interviews with SMEs (Subject Matter Experts). These individuals can provide highly specialized information. They may be the manufacturers or creators of the product.

Despite being supplied the necessary information, technical writers must be able to:

- Understand the jargon or terminology for the industry that the written material is targeted to

- Be acquainted with the tools of the trade

- Have a feel for the workflow pattern or cadence.

Chapter 89
Are You My Type?

There are three basic types of technical documentation.

1. Traditional

These are:

- Research papers
- Maintenance guides
- Repair manuals
- Articles for technical journals
- Publications
- Annual reports.

The purpose for writing these documents is to appeal to a specific audience. Your objective is to use words to simplify the complexity of the topic so your target audience has no doubt about its meaning.

2. End User Assistance

These are user manuals for:

- Medical equipment

- Computer software and hardware

- Consumer electronics like cell phones, Smartphones, iPads, iPods, televisions.

The consumer needs to know how to operate what they just bought or the company will get a lot of communication from confused and frustrated customers. This will eventually lead to lost business and a decline in profits. Since having a business is about making a profit, keeping the customer happy and able to operate the product is the main goal.

3. Marketing Communication

These are:

- Brochures

- Product catalogs

- Web content (introductory pages, about the company)

- Advertisement copy

Many times, the technical writer is required to also be able to provide graphics for the marketing.

As long as you have the ability to write an understandable, printable, and via- ble technical document, you can be a good technical user in this category. Understand the technical jargon used in the industry by the subject matter experts and translate them into layman's terms.

Your Audience

These are the people who will be using the product or service and will need to understand how it works.

Consider that they may be inexperienced about the product and since the goal is to get them to purchase the end product or service, make it easy for them to understand how it functions.

Technical writing is a way of communicating industry-related information to a specific non-industry-familiar population like explaining financial reports, or instructions on how to use something. It is vital that the technical writer has the ability to "speak" to the target audience in a way that is easy for the reader while avoiding a condescending or patronizing air.

Chapter 90
Writing Preparations

Before writing anything, you need to ask yourself two questions:

- What does my audience ALREADY KNOW about the product, service or subject matter that I am writing about?

- What does my audience WANT TO KNOW about the product, service or subject matter that I am writing about? For the first question, assume that your reader is an intelligent individual who is able to grasp complex concepts, except she or he is unfamiliar with the jargon.

For instance, if your assignment is to write the instructions on how to use a

Smartphone, assume that your reader knows the basics about using a cell phone.

The second question provides you with the "meat" of your technical document.

A typical target audience member wants to know what it is that the doohickey does and how to install it if it needs to be in- stalled. This is where technical writing is so helpful and needed.

If a product needs any type of assembly or configuration, explanations from the technical writer make the difference between a product becoming wildly popular or tossed on the use- less heap.

Pretend you don't know how to use whatever it is you are writing about. How would you explain how to use this thing to yourself? This will help in knowing what to write for someone to become knowledge- able in the usage of the product.

If the gadget has any type of alarm or noti- fication system instruct your reader on how to respond to them, e.g. what but- ton to push to override the alarm or error message, how to turn it off without losing any collected infor- mation, etc.

Tell your audience how to keep the doo- hickey operating at optimum levels. In other words, how you maintain the product and the sched- ule of doing so is discussed. Does it need to be charged periodically? Is there a recommended maintenance schedule that the buyer needs to adhere to?

You can provide this information in a book format, a pamphlet, or as an insert in the product's packaging. It all depends on the amount of information you have for your audience, and the complexity of the product itself. Some products have book- lets for each question listed above.

You can add supplemental information about the product in your technical documentation package for your audience as well, such as industry overview if the client finds this useful or important to the product's usage and attraction.

Chapter 91
The Goal of Technical Writing

The first goal of technical writing is to:

- Be organized

- Have clarity

- Correct and error-free

- Be understood

The end goal of the technical writer of course is to sell the product or service of- fered by the client. Explaining not only how to use a product but doing so in a very appealing fashion does this. For this, you need to be well versed in writing descriptions that compel the reader to buy.

The focus here is in highlighting how each feature of the product benefits the reader in such a way that makes purchasing it irresistible.

As an End User Assistance technical document writer, you need to be able to present whatever complex concept in a simplified manner. Instructions to operating a product must be broken down into a series of simple steps to follow to avoid confusing the reader from performing a specific task.

Experience in graphic art or producing illustrations via electronic media is helpful for this component in technical writing, but not imperative. Depending on the company size, you might work with a graphic artist.

Note:

A technical writer may also be called:

- Content developer

- Documentation specialist

- API writer

Chapter 92
The Process

There are four main stages in technical writing. They are:

➤ Planning

➤ Writing

➤ Delivering

➤ Archiving

The first three stages are not mutually exclusive - depending on the product. As a technical writer, you could be working on all three stages at the same time.

How can you possibly write something before planning it and deliver before writing?

If you have a product, for example, that is going to be released multiple times, you could be in the delivery stage of one version of it while writing the next, and planning the following one.

This situation happens often with high tech software - version 1.0 launches today, version 1.1 will be out in 3 months, and version 1.2 will be available in 6 months.

The only stage in technical writing that cannot happen before any of the other three is archiving. That has to happen last - for obvious reasons.

Chapter 93
It's A Plan

The Planning Stage is probably the one that takes the longest amount of time - and it should. If you have a detailed, well thought-out plan, the other phases should come together smoothly.

Take time to really understand the prod- uct or service that is being written about and featured. If the technical writer does not truly understand the product, then the reader of the content that has been written will not get it either.

So, the bottom line is - the more informa- tion you have, the better. Gather EVERYTHING there is to know about the subject matter you are assigned to write about.

While every project is going to vary, collect at least the basic information listed below:

➢ Product specifications

➢ Contract Terms and Conditions

➢ Product standards

➢ Product functional descriptions Product related software

➢ Product requirements

After you get a stack of information from your client about the product, figure out what documents you need to write. Some typical documents the client may ask you to create are:

➢ Installation Instructions/Guides Online Help Guide

➢ Product Description

➢ Operation Instructions

➢ Routine Maintenance Guide

➢ Notifications and Error Messages

➢ Tips and Helpful Hints

It is important for you, as the technical writer, to ensure that the language used in any technical documentation is consistent, clear, and concise. Talk to the person who knows the most about the product - that's the SME - Subject Matter Expert to help you work out the kinks.

Plan out a format of delivery for the technical documentation. Does it need to be printed? Should it be available via CD or online? Are all the technical documents integrated into the product's software?

Whatever delivery formats you decide on, make sure that you work out all the details. If you decided on providing a CD, how will it be labeled? Who is going to burn all the information into the disc? Will the user be able to simply load the CD and hit "Play", or will she have to download anything prior to accessing the information in the disc?

Who will print it the document you are providing? How much lead- time does the printer need? What type of binding do you want on the book?

For online access, will the audience need password or login information before viewing the documents? How is the user going to navigate the pages of information? How are the files going to be labeled?

It all sounds tedious, but the planning stage is probably the most vital. If you don't plan efficiently and effectively and don't have enough gathered information, you will end up doing more work than you need to.

3 Parts of a Good Plan

1) Sections

Include all three of these sections when planning the project:

- Table of Contents

- Devise File names

- System of saving and delivering the project

2) Utilize Templates

There is no need to reinvent the wheel. Using an appropriate template saves time and energy. By having inconsistent design construction, the reader is distracted and will have difficulty focusing on the intended content.

While the template does not need to be different for each project, it does not have to be the same, either. Try to match the template to the current style of the company so that you are "speaking in the company's voice".

3) Project Creation

- Make the instructions as simple with as few words as possible. Note how certain companies have reverted to diagrams instead of words altogether for simplicity and avoidance of language translations.

A good example of this is IKEA and their furniture assembly guides.

E.G. Avoiding verbiage, say "Connect A to Part B" or "use the Screws in packet A for the holes in Panel A"

- Do not use slang or regional colloquialisms. People may be reading these guides globally and the phrases may not be understood or worse yet have an unkind or funny message in the translation.

- Just like a cookbook lists all the needed ingredients first in the format, technical writing follows the same format by noting the needed equipment prior to the directions.

  Steps need to be explained in consecutive order. (Or one runs the risk of putting the cart before the horse)

Chapter 94
Planning Resources

There are several sources that a technical writer taps into in order to get a thorough understanding of the subject material for the content.

These are:

1) The product or service itself

   In order to really get an understanding of the product or service, you must use it first. Get the product, feel it. Turn it over. Ask yourself:

   - What is the first thing I notice about the product?

   - Is the product confusing and if so, what is it that I don't understand and need to explain?

- What benefits are there from the features seen?

- What happens when the product is tested out?

2) Descriptions and information from the inventor or creator

   There may be information or applications of the product that are not readily apparent but would be vital to the success of this product and the way it's used.

3) Professional Journals

4) Reference books

5) Old user manuals and instruction guides
   Viewing old written material that the business supports, supplies a good example of the company style or "voice of the company"

6) Competitor product

   By testing out similar products of competitors, the writer can compare them and state why the client's products are superior.

Chapter 95
Let's Write!

Now for the fun part...Writing. If you've done the planning stage well, this part of the process should be effortless.

Make a list of glossary terms as you write your technical document. When you have a little bit of downtime, research proper terms for any copyright and proprietary products that are mentioned in your technical document.

As with any and all written material, please check your spelling and proofread your work. If you use an electronic spell- checker, please have a real person who is well versed in spelling and grammar proofread the document **after** running it through spell check.

I can't tell you how many times I have read documents with common spelling errors that are usually missed by the spell checker. Misspellings such as "your" instead of "you're", "dress" instead of "address", "wore" instead of "were", "too" instead of "to"...and so on. You've seen them too - I know you have.

Mistakes like these are all too common and avoidable if you simply reread your document after using the spell check option. Read it out loud - usually you spot the mistake right away.

After reviewing your work, send it to the SME for a technical accuracy check and make the corrections promptly. Send the revised version back until the SME approves the copy.

Can You Deliver?

Delivery is probably one of the most exciting phases of technical document writing because it's where all your hard work finally comes together.

Make sure you have all the kinks worked out in terms of formatting your technical documentation for delivery.

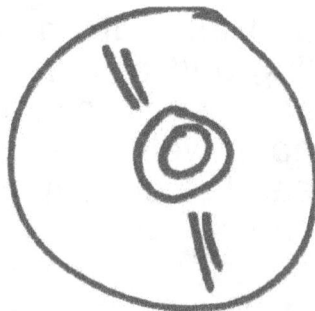

Archiving

This is where you get closure. Make sure you have the document labeled clearly - product name, number, version, date, etc. Have a separate folder for each iteration of the product. Back it up on disc.

That's it! Move on to the next project.

Chapter 96
How Do I Get Started?

OK, now that you know more about what technical writing is all about, you're just dying to get started. This is your cup of tea. Everything about it makes you tingle, and you want to know - no, NEED to know - what to do, where to go, whom to talk to - to become a technical writer.

Depending on the industry you want to specialize in, you might need a degree or at least some sort of certificate that proves your aptitude and qualifications to become a technical writer.

If you have programming knowledge and/or proven skills in graphics, these will only work in your favor. If you don't have these skills, it is advisable that you acquire them before you apply for a job as a technical writer.

Many colleges offer medical writing certification courses if you want to pursue that route. Other colleges have Technical Communications degrees and have job placement programs for their graduates.

If you have the educational background, it's recommended that you join a professional society that is related to the industry you want to specialize in as well as the Society for Technical Communication.

Joining these professional associations not only provide you with networking opportunities for possible employment, they also give you career advice, provide you access to job databases that are not listed anywhere else, and continuing education classes that will benefit you professionally.

If you are an established writer, you may not need an additional degree, but a certificate is highly recommended. It is advisable that you select a specialty or industry focus because in today's job market, a specialty marks you as an expert in the field, thus making you more market- able as a technical writer.

If you don't have the educational back- ground or any proven skills, and you STILL want to break into the niche, I won't lie to you and tell you that it will be easy, be- cause it won't be. BUT it's not impossible. People like you have done it, so it's definitely possible that you can too!

HOW???

➢ Gather letters of references and recommendations from professional as well as personal contacts. Help them write it if you have to. Some people are self-conscious about their writing ability (or perceived lack of it). Offer to write a letter and have the person review it, make adjustments, and sign it. Don't use a form letter. Write a different one for each reference.

➢ You have to be easy to get along with. I know this is not a typical techie personality trait, but the reality is, corporate America likes people who can get along and play nice with others.

➢ Work on your resume. Don't lie, but definitely find something relevant to technical writing in each and every job you have ever had.

➢ Go all out and offer to rewrite and redesign a manual. This shows that you are serious about transitioning your career into technical writing and that you have the self-confidence to succeed.

➢ Invest in a few books about technical writing, or check them out from your local library. There's even been a "Dummies" book written about technical writing. Other books to consider are:

• Handbook of Technical Writing, 9th Ed (Gerald Alred)

- Chicago Manual of Style - this might be in the 15th or 16th edition. It's a copywriter's standard reference tool.

- The Elements of Style by Strunk and White. I've had my worn out copy for 25 years now, and I still use it. I'm sure there are many more books out there - in the specialty that you choose too. I've just listed some basic ones. You can look it up online and you'll find a library full of books on Amazon, Barnes and Noble, and other booksellers.

Chapter 97
Versatility

In deciding upon a career as a technical writer, one has many choices.

1) Employment status

Freelance contractor:

Advantages:

☐ Less supervision

☐ Can pick and choose the projects of interest

☐ Get greater tax deductions

Disadvantages:

☐ Must constantly be marketing oneself to get assignments

☐ No job security

☐ No benefits like health and life insurance provided

On-site hired employee

Advantages:

☐ Job stability

☐ Provided Health insurance

☐ Enrolled in a pension plan

Disadvantages:

☐ Vacations and time off must be approved

☐ No choice in projects assigned

☐ May have to work within idiosyncrasies of bureaucracy.

Departments looking for Technical Writers

- Research and Development

- Information Architecture

- Publications

- Document Management

- User assistance

- ➤ While every project is going to vary, collect at least the basic information listed below in the Planning Stage:

    - ➤ Product specifications

    - ➤ Contract Terms and Conditions Product standards

    - ➤ Product functional descriptions Product related software

    - ➤ Product requirements

- ➤ If you have the educational background, it's recommended that you join a professional society that is related to the industry you want to specialize in as well as the Society for Technical Communication.

    Joining these professional associations not only provide you with networking opportunities for possible employment, they also give you career advice, provide you access to job databases that are not listed anywhere else, and continuing education classes that will benefit you professionally.

Chapter 98
Review

Answer the questions and review topics

1) Name a professional association that you can join as a technical writer. What are some benefits of joining?

2) What are 2 questions you need to ask yourself before writing technical documents?

3) What are the 3 types of technical documentation?

4) Give an example or two of the first type of technical documentation you listed in #3.

5) Give an example or two of the second type of technical documentation you listed in #3.

6) Give an example or two of the third type of technical documentation you listed in #3.

7) What basic information should you collect in the Planning Stage?

8) What are the 4 stages of the technical documentation writing process?

9) T/F: You need to be a great writer to break into the technical writing niche

10) T/F: You can break into the technical writing niche without having a degree.

GET YOUR LATEST EZINE
NEWS & VIEWS ONLINE
(AND GET ON MY LIST)

Chapter 99
Editorials vs. Advertorials

Editorials

Similar to essays, editorials reflect the personal beliefs or opinions regarding a certain topic that the writer feels very strongly about. Frequently, it relates to a current event or incident that has recently occurred.

Basically, editorials reflect not only the facts but also the opinions that regard a specific topic in a short and sweet manner. It includes the editor's dissection of the particular subject. The main purpose of an editorial is to help people gain insight into their social, economic and cultural conditions of life's surroundings.

Advertorials

On the other side of this coin are Advertorials. An Advertorial is a marketing tool, written like an article that you would read in any newspaper or magazine, except it is only about you and your company or product. There is no second opinion! Despite the presentation and content seeming to be a news article, the advertorial is YOUR story told in YOUR own way.

Editorial Vs. Advertorial

Since the publication where you submit an editorial has control over what is printed, the article or editorial is printed on the whim of the editor. It is chosen because it is interesting and newsworthy.

Certain uninteresting parts may be omitted, and other, more newsworthy sections may be covered in greater detail. The publication has control over what they want published.

That's the reason why many companies send generic press releases and pitch them to multiple publications – to play the odds that someone, somewhere, may find this news worthy of publication.

On the other hand, an advertorial is actually an advertisement that is paid by the company for submission although it is subtle since the presentation and con- tent does seem like a newsworthy story instead of an advertisement. It attracts or induces potential customers to the company paying for the advertorial.

Some may argue that the publication loses its objective credibility by printing and accepting payment for obviously biased company messaging. However, companies are always looking for new and creative ways to spread their message and to ex- pand their market segment.

Advertorials are a great way for them to garner publicity. If you look at it as an ad – albeit camouflaged - then it's not damaging to the publication's credibility – It's just ad.

Chapter 100
Editorials

Many people are unaware of the fact that writing an article is incredibly different from writing an editorial. Articles that are printed in newspapers and magazines (online included) are just collected news and data that come in and selectively are sorted out and displayed. An Editorial, on the other hand, is a cautiously created piece of work.

Editorials are written to reflect the opinion of the periodical. An editorial is also known as an opinion piece, which is usually written by senior staff and the publisher of a newspaper or magazine.

Many different print publications actually print editorials, and/or letters to the editor.

In major newspapers such as the New York Times, for instance, editorials are found under the heading 'opinion'. On occasion, editorials are also found in the form of cartoons – like Garry Trudeau's Doonesbury.

A newspaper's editorial board decides and evaluates the most important issues about which their readers need to hear different opinions.

An editorial is just a way for reporters to give their own *personal* opinion instead of the even-handed method that's used by the newspaper, the most important things to remember while writing an editorial is the proper writing style.

Of course you can include your personal opinion, but you have to have precise and easy to understand writing. If you learn the right way, editorial writing isn't very difficult.

Chapter 101
Choosing a Topic

When trying to decide on a topic, providing your readers with content they can relate to is essential.

Although not all editorials are written in preference to one side of a current issue, they are typically written in a way that will influence the reader to think and act in a similar way to the writer.

Three Qualities for an Editorial

A well-written editorial typically contains the following three qualities:

1. It informs the reader about the existence of a particular issue, and explains it in a way that the reader understands the factors leading to the issue.

2. It gets the reader involved in the story and encourages the reader to take action in one form or another.

3. It praises the newsworthy person or event.

There is a multitude of ways that you can create a well-written editorial, and if you search online, you'll probably find millions of results for "editorial writing". **No matter what you write about, all well-written editorials have four main parts.**

These are:

- A current newsworthy issue or event.

- Details supporting your viewpoint.

- The other side of the story – highlight the weaknesses of the opposing side without badmouthing or attacking.

- Offer a solution and proof to why this is the best possible solution to the issue at hand.

Chapter 102
The Fast Five

Below is a checklist for you to use.

Step 1: Make sure that you choose some type of current event to brain- storm about. In order for your editorial to be good, you must address an issue or topic that is on the public's mind RIGHT NOW, before it will ever get to print.

Step 2: Start with a thesis! It doesn't have to be stated right away but just like in most writing your thesis is the foundation for your editorial piece. The thesis helps present a clear understanding that you are taking on a particular subject.

Step 3: Use facts to support your view- point. Do not use hypothetical situations. The more proof you have to back up your opinion, the more supporters you will gain. Try doing a little light research on your topic just enough for you to understand and make use of statistics and or data that you find as support for your position.

Step 4: Support your facts with emotional or social appeal to your readers. A lot of editorials use persuasive language, and because of it editorials often get read more than news stories do. Be Creative! A headline that reads "Breaking the Ice" just might get more readers attention than a news headline like "An Icelandic Whaling Ship Sinks". Therefore readers can actually follow along more easily when your piece includes direct and personal touches.

Step 5: Get involved with others. There may be a time when your paper might want a group written editorial to help repre- sent the combined opinion of you and your colleagues. If it's possible you can even get together and come up with a thesis. If it turns out to not be ideal you might have to go in for it alone, and take turns writing the editorial.

Chapter 103
Advertorials

The best way to describe this marketing tool is that an advertorial is a piece of advertising made to look like content.

Compared to most advertisements, the advertorial needs a different tone. It has to be less promotional and more "newsy." Basically an advertorial is an ad that's written to look and sound like an editorial.

With any typical advertisement, you aim for the ad to jump off the page. But with an advertorial, you want the ad to sort of blend in, just as if it's just another article.

It can be difficult for many writers to switch from a promotional tone to a more newsy tone which is why there is a 7 step process listed below to help you grasp the concept of writing an advertorial.

Seven Steps to Writing an Advertorial

Step 1: Start brainstorming the product to help you find ideas for your story- line. When you're able to know a product inside and out - its features, benefits and modes of utilization - you are better able to fit it into an everyday context.

Step 2: Choose your everyday setting for your storyline. It's best to use ideas and surroundings that your audience is familiar with. As an example, if you are selling a new cleaning detergent, you may want to set your story in either the kitchen or garage in a home where the home's residents would typically find themselves cleaning.

Step 3: Go ahead – don't hesitate to include action and dialog into your story. People tend to remember things in different ways because of different learning styles. Because of this, the well-written and effective advertorial must be multi- dimensional and appeal to the visual as well as the auditory learner.

Step 4: Ensure that your advertorial has a beginning, middle and an end just as a story does. Even though an aver- age advertorial is a little less than 800 words, that doesn't mean there is no logical sequence of events that can't be concluded. An easy way to remember this is that a complete story is easier to remember than an unfinished thought.

Step 5: Keep a ten- foot pole between you and discussing the price of the product and other topics that the reader might consider out of context or out of character for the particular publication. For instance, when writing an advertorial, don't come up with a catchy jingle or write overt marketing "buzz words". The idea of an advertorial is its editorial nature, meaning that contact information such as a website discreetly noted at the end of the story has much more appeal than "MBA-talk".

Step 6: Remember to include and explain complex product details within the story- line. Even though an advertorial entertains while it informs, complicated products may require a lot more attention than others. Understanding the features as well as seeing their benefits is VERY important to a customer.

Step 7: Take case studies and testimonials into consideration as support for documentation to the storyline.

Remember that when an advertorial is written well, it will bring in a lot of money for you or your client, thus increasing the demand for your writing. A poorly written advertorial will fizzle and flop, and you will be as forgotten as the ineffective piece.

Chapter 104
Key Points

Editorials

- ➤ Keep your topic relevant

- ➤ Use personal opinion

- ➤ Feel free to use emotion but in a limited manner

- ➤ Use persuasive language

- Get your facts straight

- Try to be entertaining

Advertorials

- Know EVERYTHING about your product

- Make sure your storyline is something that your audience can relate to and or is familiar with

- Include action and dialogue

- Have a beginning, middle, and end.

- Steer clear of unnecessary content

- Include and explain complex product details

Chapter 105
Review

Review and answer the questions to see how much you've learned.

Questions:

1. What is the difference between an Editorial and an Advertorial?

2. When choosing a topic what is most important to take into consideration and why?

3. When writing an editorial who decides what information is most important to their readers?

4. Why would you want an advertorial to blend in as if it is just another article?

5. What is step 4 to writing an advertorial and why is it so crucial?

6. What is the first step to writing an editorial?

7. Give an example of a headline you might use for an editorial compared to that of a newspaper headline.

8. List two steps to writing an editorial.

9. In your own words, what is an Editorial?

10. Sum up exactly what you believe an Advertorial is without looking back at the text.

NO NEED TO
SLAVE ALL NIGHT
I'LL HELP YOU!

Overwhelmed? No worries! Outsource your writing projects.

We would be happy to do it for you!

Contact: Support@CompleteContent Package. com

Having a mastery of the types of content writing discussed in this book will enable you to promote yourself and others, achieving a high level of success.

If you neither have the time nor inclination to delve into content writing for your website and business, you needn't worry... Outsource it!

We would be happy to do it for you!

Contact support@CompleteContent Package. com for advice or help with your projects.